GREAT MYSTERIES

Noah's Ark

OPPOSING VIEWPOINTS®

Look for these and other exciting *Great Mysteries: Opposing Viewpoints* books:

GREAT MYSTERIES

Noah's Ark

OPPOSING VIEWPOINTS®

by Patricia Kite

Greenhaven Press, Inc.   P.O. Box 289009, San Diego, California 92128-9009

Kite, Patricia, 1940-
  Noah's ark.

  (Great mysteries : opposing viewpoints)
  Bibliography: p.
  Includes index.
  Summary: Presents opposing viewpoints on the legendary Ark and Flood, discussing research done to prove one way or another if there is a historical basis to this "great mystery."
    1. Noah's ark—Juvenile literature. 2. Deluge—Juvenile literature. [1. Noah's ark. 2. Deluge]
I. Title II. Series: Great mysteries (Saint Paul, Minn.)
BS658.K53 1989   222'.11095   89-11635
ISBN 0-89908-073-1

© Copyright 1989 by Greenhaven Press, Inc.
Produced by Carnival Enterprises, Minneapolis, MN
Every effort has been made to trace owners of copyright material.

This book is dedicated to my parents,
Oscar and Sarah Padams,
who allowed a curious child to be curious.

Contents

Introduction

This book is written for the curious–those who want to explore the mysteries that are everywhere. To be human is to be constantly surrounded by wonderment. How do birds fly? Are ghosts real? Can animals and people communicate? Was King Arthur a real person or a myth? Why did Amelia Earhart disappear? Did history really happen the way we think it did? Where did the world come from? Where is it going?

Great Mysteries: Opposing Viewpoints books are intended to offer the reader an opportunity to explore some of the many mysteries that both trouble and intrigue us. For the span of each book, we want the reader to feel he or she is a scientist investigating the extinction of the dinosaurs, an archaeologist searching for clues to the origin of the great Egyptian pyramids, a psychic detective testing the existence of ESP.

One thing all mysteries have in common is that there is no ready answer. Often there are *many* answers, but none on which even the majority of authorities agrees. *Great Mysteries: Opposing Viewpoints* books introduce intriguing views of the experts, allowing the reader to participate in their explorations, their theories, and their disagreements as they try to explain the mysteries of our world.

But most readers won't want to stop here. These *Great Mysteries: Opposing Viewpoints* aim to stimulate the reader's curiosity. Although truth is often impossible to discover, the search is fascinating. It is up to the reader to examine the evidence, to decide whether the answer is there—or to explore further.

"Penetrating so many secrets, we cease to believe in the unknowable. But there it sits nevertheless, calmly licking its chops."

H.L. Mencken, American essayist

Prologue

Noah Builds an Ark

"In the central part of Armenia stands an exceeding large and high mountain, upon which, it is said, the Ark of Noah rested, and for this reason it is termed the "Mountain of the Ark."

Marco Polo, A.D. 1300

The biblical book of Genesis, chapters 6-9, says that when humanity became wicked and violent and would not reform, God became angry. There was only one really good man, and that was Noah.

"Build an ark," God said to Noah, "and waterproof it. Make it three stories high and put compartments in it for living space and animals of different sizes." God told Noah there would be a great flood. All living things not in the ark would be destroyed.

Noah did as he was told. He built an ark according to God's detailed directions. It was large like a ship, but shaped more like a long box. Noah made rooms for his wife, his three sons and their wives, animals, and food storage. He also tried to warn the townspeople, but they laughed at him and continued their wicked ways.

According to Genesis, it took Noah over 100 years to build the ark. He was 600 years old when he finished. Then God told Noah to bring on board the ark two of each kind of animal, including cattle, reptiles, and birds. He was to bring a male and a female of each kind, so that when the time came, they could

"And rain fell upon the earth forty days and forty nights." (Gen. 7:12). The Flood, as depicted by Masseot Abaquesne in the sixteenth century.

"We only played Bible games with these animals, yet we never tired of arranging them in pairs, to walk in a long procession with Noah and his family at decent intervals, round the dining-room table. We sorted them out, and found the partners, and argued about the precedence of different animals, or the species of the dogs."

Alison Uttley, *Ambush of Young Days*

"If animals really were created in pairs, how would they have survived predators? Wouldn't the first pair of lions have eaten the first pair of deer, then feasted upon the first pair of zebra, then gobbled up all the other weaker animals as well, until the lions themselves starved to death?"

Jared Diamond, *Discover* magazine

reproduce and repopulate earth. Noah did as he was told. Then he closed the door of the ark and waited for seven days.

Suddenly, water poured down from the sky and the "fountains of the great deep burst forth." First the low ground was covered. Then the water rose higher, uprooting trees and lifting big stones. It rained for forty days and forty nights, the water rising until it covered the mountain.

Noah's ark floated on the water's surface for 110 days. Whenever he looked out, Noah saw only water.

Then the wind began to blow, and the flood waters began to recede. The rain stopped and the "fountains of the deep" were closed.

The water kept decreasing for another 114 days. Then the ark came to rest "on the mountains of Ararat." Noah let loose a raven to see if there was any place it could land. But the bird returned. Seven days later Noah sent out a dove. It too came back because there was no place to land. Noah sent the dove out a second time. This time it returned with an olive leaf in its beak. To Noah, this meant the waters had retreated to a level where hardy olive trees had begun to grow again. The third time the dove went out, it never returned, for it had a found a place to live. Noah knew that someplace not far away, the ground surface was dry.

Noah and his family and all the animals left the ark. They had been aboard it a year. Only these eight people survived the Flood, but in time they increased to many thousands. God promised Noah that he would never again destroy every living creature.

What became of the ark after Noah and his family left it is never mentioned in the Bible and is a mystery still.

Ark hunters, such as David Fasold, have climbed Mt. Ararat for decades seeking Noah's Ark.
Note the boat-shaped formation in the middle of the photograph.
Is this where it came to rest?

One

The Past is Unearthed

The greatest archaeological hunt in history started only 150 years ago. The searchers are not looking for gold and silver, although they occasionally find them. They are not looking for jewels. The are biblical archaeologists searching for evidence of the biblical past.

Archaeologists are hole diggers. They study ancient relics, tools, and bones–scraps of past human life and activities. Nothing gives them more pleasure than carefully putting together tiny bits of pottery or mysterious fragments from a writing tablet found at the site of a dig or excavation.

One of the greatest archeological mysteries is the tale of Noah. Could Noah's Flood really have happened the way it is described in the Bible? Biblical archaeologists have sought ways to find out.

Biblical archaeologists need many special skills. They must know the history of people living in biblical times. They must study the geography of the past as well as the present. And they must understand the results of past excavations. These archaeologists must also be language experts, knowing Hebrew, as

Opposite page: A Babylonian account of the flood is inscribed on this clay tablet, part of the Epic of Gilgamesh. This Assyrian version dates from the seventh century B.C.

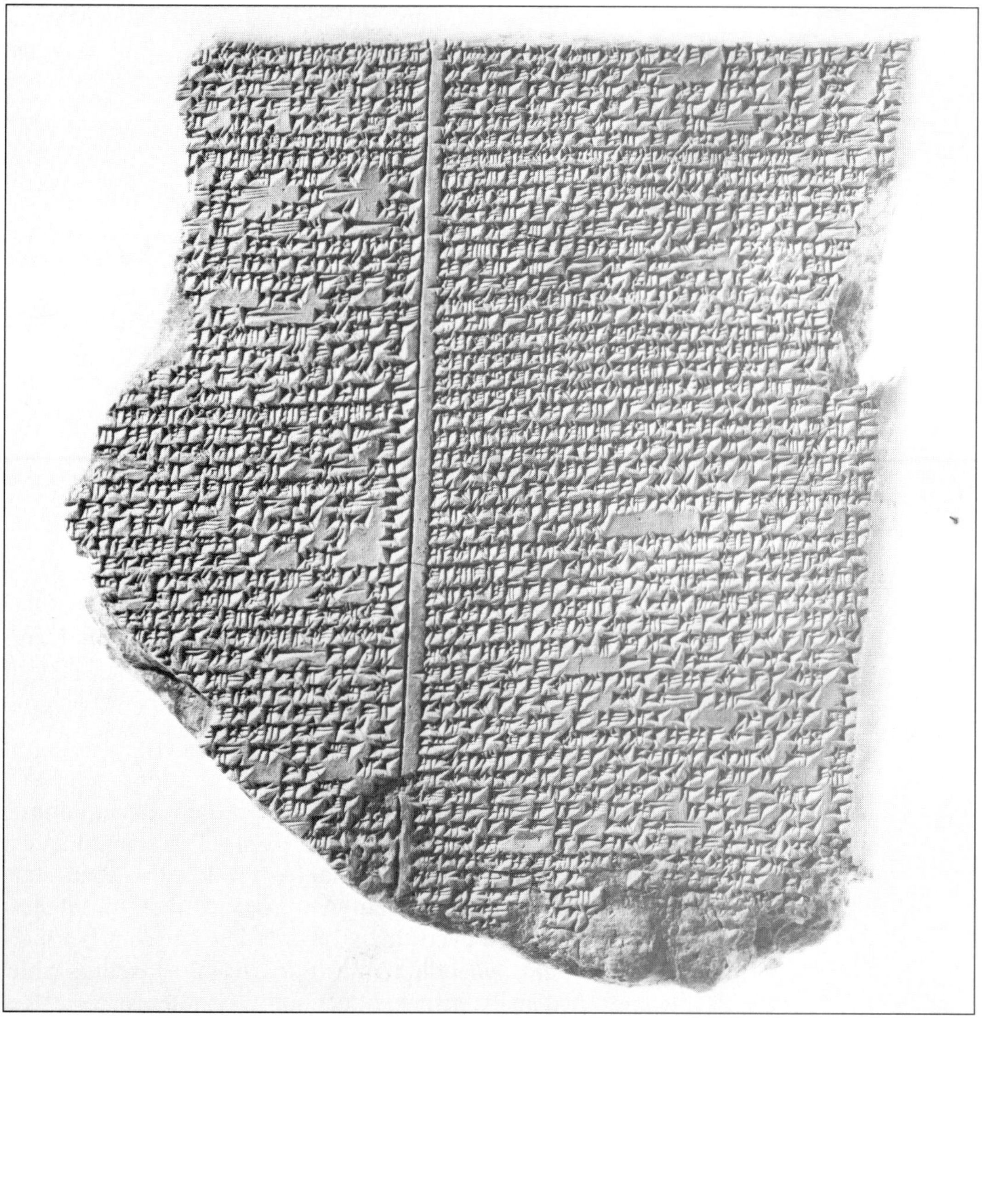

George Smith, the man who discovered an account of a great flood on cuneiform tablets from Mesopotamia.

well as some ancient Sumerian, Egyptian, Aramaic, Accadian, Ugarit, Latin, and Greek. All of these languages come from the Middle Eastern area where most biblical history took place.

Cuneiform Writing From the Past

Among the most important treasures to biblical archaeologists are clay tablets, even tiny fragments of clay tablets. Many of these are covered with cuneiform, an ancient form of writing.

Before paper was invented, people used a special chisel to make web-shaped characters in soft clay. These cuneiform letters told stories and transmitted messages. The clay was then baked until it hardened to preserve the message.

Wars and natural disasters destroyed so much of past culture that for thousands of years nobody could figure out what the cuneiform writings meant. But gradually archaeologists and language experts pieced together the language maze, first letter by letter, then word by word. Those strange-looking markings often tell very dramatic tales.

George Smith Discovers Noah

One of the most fantastic biblical archeological stories resulted from an accidental discovery in 1872 by a man who was not a trained archaeologist. George Smith, an apprentice at a London money engraving firm, had a hobby. He liked to read about and look at ancient Assyrian artifacts or objects. Smith enjoyed this so much that he spent his lunch hours and holidays at the British Museum, which had an extensive collection of such items.

Smith was there so often that the person in charge noticed him, and eventually they chatted. When the museum needed a careful person to repair some broken clay tablets, the job was offered to Smith. What could be better than working at what you love best?

There were 25,000 clay tablets, dug up from the war-destroyed library of King Assurbanipal. He lived from 668-626 B.C in a city called Nineveh. These tablets had been quite carelessly handled by the excavation diggers, who considered them "decorated pottery." Heaped into baskets, they travelled thousands of miles, many of them breaking into smaller pieces on the journey to the British Museum.

Smith quit his engraving job and was soon a full-time museum employee. He was still there ten years later, putting together clay tablets by color and shape, much like working on a jigsaw puzzle. He laboriously copied the cuneiform language signs from the clay to paper. Doing that for a decade, Smith also taught himself to read and translate the signs. Around him, archaeologists talked, travelled, and wrote long papers about their great discoveries. Smith, the reader and translator who loved stories of the Near East and its history, had never been anyplace near the site of his tablets.

One afternoon, while continuing his cuneiform copy work, Smith came upon half a tablet with a

This illustration from an eleventh-century French manuscript shows Noah's family and the animals leaving the ark after the Deluge.

story that seemed quite easy to understand, unlike most of his other readings. Why was that? Because the tale was so familiar. It told about a ship landing on the mountains of Nisir. It mentioned a dove being sent out, not finding a place to land, and returning to the ship. What was this all about? Could it be the story of Noah's Ark from the Bible?

The Assyrian and Sumerian Noahs

Noah wasn't called Noah, in this tale, but Utnapishtim. And there were some other differences, but they were minor. Excitedly, Smith told museum officials about his discovery—and the archaeological world went wild. Now there might be proof that Noah's Flood really happened.

Smith began wondering whether, beneath the grounds of ancient Assyria, there might also "lay, together with older copies of this Deluge text, other legends and histories." Because of all the newspaper publicity about his discovery, he was now a public hero. That same publicity brought him enough money to go to Nineveh, in Iraq, in search of other tablets.

Months later, Smith was under the hot Middle Eastern sun among piles of dirt, excavation equipment, hundreds of scattered and broken clay tablets, and bricks of a buried city. He was looking for a needle in a haystack: a piece of clay containing more information about the Deluge or Flood story. An impossible task, surely.

One week after Smith arrived at the Nineveh ruins, he reached down and picked up a fragment from the day's digging. There it was! The poem-story, now known as the Gilgamesh Epic, told of a universal, or world-wide, Deluge which closely paralleled Noah and the Flood. "I am the first man to read this text after 2,000 years of oblivion!" Smith exclaimed. Smith left Nineveh shortly afterward but returned two years later at age 35. This time he had a crew of 600, and recovered more than three thousand impor-

Famed archaeologist Sir Leonard Woolley, whose excavations proved the existence of an ancient city named in the Bible—Ur.

tant clay tablet fragments. But instead of solving the Deluge mystery once and for all, Smith's discoveries only opened up another Pandora's box of questions.

Following Smith's momentous discovery, many other archaeologists began to study Nineveh and neighboring sites, seeking more clues toward understanding the exciting Deluge story. From 1889-1900, excavations at Nippur in Mesopotamia (also part of Iraq) unearthed a Sumerian version of Noah's Flood, dating before the Babylonian Gilgamesh. Here the hero was named Ziusudra. Other versions also turned up in the widespread and painstaking excavations, with hero's names such as Xisuthros, Ubaratutu, Khasistrata, and Baisbarata. But in all the discoveries, the general Deluge story was quite similar. All described one universal Flood, the end of humanity, and its renewal.

Sir Leonard Woolley Digs Up the Flood

In the late 1920s, Sir Leonard Woolley, a world-famous British archaeologist, was trying to find the starting point of Sumerian civilization. His method: digging a shaft straight down through the ruins of one of the most ancient cities in the world, Ur, in lower Mesopotamia.

When Woolley first started digging he found all sorts of old items. These were ordinary items, such as tools and ornaments, showing human workmanship.

Then he discovered the "Royal Cemetery," groups of burial vaults placed one on top of another. The tombs furthest down took him back to 2800 B.C. Was this the bottom? The stubborn Woolley kept going. He found artifacts from 3000 B.C. These bits and pieces of the past, which would have looked like trash to an amateur, were like gold to Woolley.

Suddenly, the layers of pottery fragments, building rubble, and clay tablet pieces stopped. Instead there was nothing but "clean water-laid clay," or what we simply call "mud." But where did this come from?

Excited, Woolley continued his search down through the earth. Only after going through eleven feet of nothing but this soft mud did the crew find more pottery and other artifacts. But this didn't answer Woolley's question about the mud that lay between one civilization and another. It was obvious that some natural catastrophe had destroyed the older civilization, and covered it with mud. Could this possibly be proof of the Bible story? Woolley thought so. "I have found the Flood!" he announced to the world.

After further analysis, he concluded that the flood waters covering the area were about 25 feet deep. According to biblical interpreters, this was almost the same depth as mentioned in Genesis, "fifteen cubits upward did the waters prevail." (One cubit is

Woolley explores the great trench at Ur.

The legend of a man or family that survives a catastrophic flood by boat is told all around the world

estimated by scholars to equal seventeen to twenty-one inches.)

Dating the flood deposit at Ur around 4000 B.C., Woolley was convinced he had discovered the historical reality behind the Flood legend. The skeptics who thought a universal Deluge was a myth were forced to reconsider their beliefs.

More Than One Flood

Just as Woolley's discovery seemed to be shutting the door on any further Deluge debate, other archaeologists stopped it from from closing. Large mud deposits were soon found at other sites. If this had been the same mud as the Ur mud, scholars felt it would be just about positive proof that the Flood story was true.

But the evidence didn't match. The Flood deposits at the cities of Kish and Fara in Mesopotamia were left at different times than the Nineveh site. To make matters more complex, further poking about demonstrated that the Ur mud layer didn't cover the entire city, as Woolley first thought. Surely it would have, if it was left over from the Great Flood. The debate flared anew.

Two

Why Are There Different Flood Tales?

Flood stories have come to us through legend and folktales for at least three thousand years. The legends, although not identical, often have common themes: All people and animals were destroyed by a great flood except those surviving on a sailing vessel or high mountain peak.

The Biblical Version

Biblical descriptions of Noah's Flood are part of the book of Genesis in the Old Testament, written about 147 B.C., or 1,475 years "before Christ." Noah's Flood is believed to have occurred about 4,300 years ago. But there are those who think a universal Flood could have occurred a long time before that. There are several different translations of the Bible, and wording varies a bit. But as a whole, the Catholic, Protestant, and Jewish versions of Noah's story are all similar to the story that opens this book.

Pre-Biblical Flood Tales

There are more than 200 flood legends known from ancient tribes and civilizations. Others may yet be found or translated from ancient languages. Some legends are remarkably similar, despite the tribes and

Opposite page: "He blotted out every living thing that was upon the face of the ground, man and animals and creeping things and birds of the air; they were blotted out from the earth." (Gen. 7:23)

ILVVIVQVADRAGITADIEB;SVPRAETOVINDECICVBITISALCIOR
VPOMSMONTES;CVQCOSPREETOISCROSVPRAEMISNOECO
BА̄

VITADEVPOKSRAMOLIVEIORE·ETITELLEXNOEQCESSASETО̄.DILVVII·
·PONAMARCVINNVBIB;   ETERITSIGNVFEDERIS
                                      TNOSITVLRA
                                      AQVE
                                      OLLVVI¯

OPVLITHOLOCVSVSDRO   POLVVI

countries having no known contact with each other. Other stories are quite individualistic.

Sumerian

The oldest written records known come from the city of Nippur in ancient Mesopotamia. Nippur, located along the midpoint of the Euphrates River, was the area's political and religious center. The people were called Sumerians.

A broken Sumerian clay tablet, dating before 2000 B.C. and perhaps as early as 3400 B.C., was found during archaeological excavations in Nippur. It gives an incomplete account of the Great Flood. Even the small fragments have a story quite similar to Noah's: "After for seven days and seven nights, The Flood had swept over the land, And the huge boat had been tossed about by the windstorms on the great waters."

In the Sumerian story, an assembly of the gods decreed a Flood should take place. But Nintu, the goddess of birth, and Enki, the god of wisdom, did not agree that all humanity should be destroyed. Enki decided to save Ziusudra, a very wise and good man who paid careful attention to the gods. In a dream, Ziusudra was warned that a flood would be sent to destroy humanity. He was then given an escape plan. The rest of this Sumerian story, which scholars assume deals with the construction of a boat, has never been found.

Babylonian

The Babylonians, and later the Assyrians, followed the Sumerians, adopting many Sumerian religious customs and beliefs. Much of the knowledge we now have about these people was written by the Babylonian historian Berossus, whose writings were copied by later historians. This copying has led to theories that later versions of a Great Flood came from the writings of Berossus and perhaps other historians.

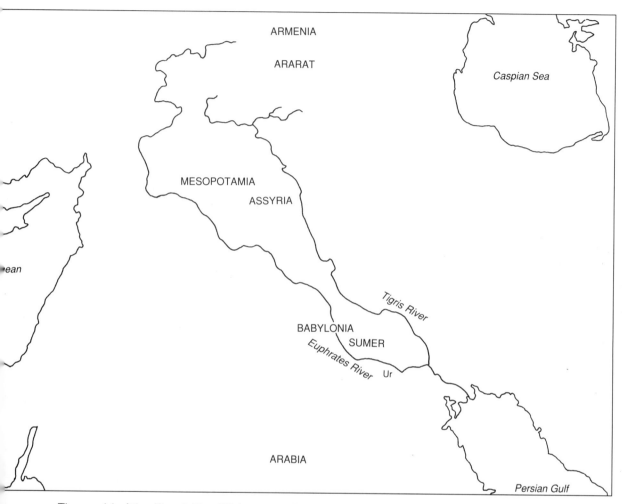

The world of the Flood. The Bible states that Noah's Ark came to rest on the mountains of Ararat, now within the borders of Turkey.

The Assyrians knew of the Epic of Gilgamesh, where a hero who is part god and part human has many adventures and learns of the Flood from an immortal named Utnapishtim.

The Gilgamesh epic, the Babylonian story-poem discovered by George Smith, dates back to about the seventh century B.C. In it, King Gilgamesh, part god and part human, seeks a way to live forever. He hears that Utnapishtim, a Babylonian, is supposedly immortal, and goes to look for him.

After surviving many dangers along the way, Gilgamesh meets Utnapishtim, who tells him the story of the Great Flood, and how he was given immortality after surviving it. "Even the gods were terror-stricken at the deluge. For six days and six nights, the wind blew, and the deluge and the tempest overwhelmed the land."

This Flood, according to the eleventh tablet of the Gilgamesh Epic, was ordered by "the great gods," particularly the powerful air-god Enlil. No particular reason for the destruction was offered, although the story hints that humanity was not behaving itself. Originally all living things were targeted for destruction. However, the god Ea, whose job it was to take care of humanity, objected to the scheme.

In a dream, Ea warned Utnapishtim to "tear down thy house, build a ship! Cause to go up into the ship the seed of all living creatures. The ship which thou shalt build, its measurements shall be accurately measured; its width and its length shall be equal."

The ship was coated in a waterproof substance called *pitch*. Its floor covered one *iku*, or about an acre. The walls were 120 cubits high, and each side was 120 cubits long (about 200 feet high and wide), making a square. The ship was seven stories high and had nine sections.

When the Flood arrived, the Gilgamesh author relates, "In the evening the leader of the storm caused a destructive rain to rain down. I viewed the appearance of the weather; the weather was frightful to behold. I entered the ship and closed the door."

This boat, according to the tablets, survived six days and nights, stopping the seventh day on Mount Nisir, a site about 350 miles from Mount Ararat, where many believe is the landing site of Noah's Ark.

The discovery of the Gilgamesh Epic led many people, including historian Sir James Frazer, to wonder whether the Genesis account of Noah's Flood was partially based on the ancient Babylonian epic. There were certainly many similarities, as already mentioned, in the portions about the Flood.

Author John Clement Whitcomb, a contemporary scholar, says the similarities are merely coincidence. The Gilgamesh Epic couldn't be the precursor of the Flood story in Genesis, he feels, because Genesis is an original story based on the word of God.

Let us look at some other stories, many of which were collected by historian Sir James Frazer in his book *Folklore in the Old Testament*. Most of the people no longer exist as they did when the stories originated. These stories were passed from one generation to another via word of mouth, often with special persons acting as official tale-tellers or historians within the group. Now the only records we have

"We will not try to prove the Bible. We accept it as God's Word and believe it in its most straightforward and literal interpretation."

Tim La Haye and John Morris, *The Ark on Ararat*

"The discovery of the Sumerian epic, with its combined accounts of the creation and deluge, renders it highly probable that the narratives of the early history of the world found in Genesis did not originate with the Semites, but were borrowed by them from the older civilized people."

Historian Sir James Frazer, *Folklore in the Old Testament*

of their myths and legends come from missionaries and scholars who sought out the tale-tellers and made detailed records. It is interesting to note that these tales come from all over the world, not just from the Holy Land explored by archaeologists such as George Smith and Sir Leonard Woolley.

Other Tales

From Lithuania, in Europe, comes a story about Pramzimas, chief of the ancient gods. One day, Pramzimas looked from the window of his heavenly house onto humanity. He saw nothing but war and injustice. Angered, Pramzimas sent two giants, Water and Wind, to destroy the earth. They caused such damage that after twenty days and twenty nights, there was very little of the world left. Only a few peo-

The voyage of Noah's Ark as imagined by a Jewish painter, Malkah Zeldis.

ple and some animals survived on the highest mountaintop, and it looked as if they too might be lost. But Pramzimas happened to look out of his heavenly window again. He was eating nuts at the time and knocked some nutshells off the heavenly window sill. One huge nutshell fell onto the high mountaintop and all the stranded people got into it. This boat rescued them from the rising waters. Later, Pramzimas looked out again, decided he was no longer angry, and told Wind and Water to stop their damage.

According to the Munda tribe of southwestern Bengal, the god Sing Boga was sorry he had created humanity, since they would not "wash themselves, or work, or do anything but dance and sing" constantly. So Sing Bonga sent down a shower of *Sengle-Daa,* or fire-water, from heaven. Only a boy and a girl survived. Sing Bonga took pity and sent the snake Lurbing, in the shape of a rainbow, to hold up the showers. From the Santals, another Bengalese aboriginal tribe, comes this verse: "Seven days and seven nights it rained fire-rain, Where were you, ye two human beings? Where did you pass the time?"

There are several Hawaiian stories of a great flood. Many were collected, beginning in 1822, by the Reverend William Ellis, who was very interested in island history. He heard his first flood story when he started to preach in Hawaii. Part of his teaching was a sermon on Noah's Ark. After one sermon, Hawaiian natives came to him and said they also had a flood legend. "They said," Ellis wrote, "that their fathers told them that all the land had once been overflowed by the sea, except a small peak on the top of Mouna-Kea, where two human beings were preserved from the destruction that overtook the rest." But the natives had never before heard of a ship or of Noah.

Mexico has many flood tales, differing somewhat by region. In Michoacan, a state in southwest

"We...find it difficult to recognize in the diverse, often quaint, childish, or grotesque stories of a great flood, the human copies of a single divine original."

Historian Sir James Frazer, *Folklore in the Old Testament*

"All the same, legends do not appear from nowhere; they too have their beginning in time and space."

Archaeologist G.S. Wegener, *6,000 Years of the Bible*

Many tribal peoples around the world—from North and South America to Indonesia and the Polynesian islands of the Pacific ocean—share flood tales of one kind or another.

Mexico, the natives say that when the flood waters began to rise, Tezpi, a religious man, and his wife and children, got into a great vessel. They took with them animals and seeds of many kinds to enable them to replant the world following the flood. When the waters went down, Tezpi sent out a vulture to find land.

More Tribal Tales

In the tribal tales of the Cherokee Indians of the southeastern United States, the coming of a flood was told by a dog to his master. "You must build a boat," the dog said, "and put in it all that you would save; for a great rain is coming that will flood the land."

The Tlingit tribe of northwestern Alaska told of a great flood which, driven by wind, covered all dwelling places. The Tlingits saved themselves by tying several boats together to make a great raft.

They floated on this, huddling together for warmth under a tent until Anodjium, a magician, ordered the sea to be calm and the flood to recede.

Friar Geronimo Boscana, author of *Chinigchinich*, wrote, "The Acagchemem Indians, near San Juan Capistrano in Southern California, were not entirely destitute of a knowledge of the universal Deluge, but how, or from whence, they received the same, I could never understand. Some of their songs refer to it; and they have a tradition that, at a time very remote, the sea began to swell and roll in upon the plains, and fill the valleys, until it had covered the mountains; and thus nearly all the human race and animals were destroyed, excepting a few, who had resorted to a very high mountain which the waters did not reach."

The Carayas, an extremely isolated Brazilian Indian tribe, have a great flood legend among their many stories of ancient times. The Carayas believed that all water flowed out of calabash gourds, which were jugs carried by the god Anatiua. Offended by Caraya behavior, he broke the calabashes, one after another, until the waters rose. Only a few people survived, and these were on the highest mountaintop.

The Carayas differed from all their neighboring tribes in the Amazon region, in customs as well as physical appearance. Their language is apparently unrelated to any other known language. Where could their story have come from if it didn't originate as a recounting from generation to generation of a true happening?

According to a Greek legend from the fifth century B.C., the great god Zeus became annoyed at humanity. He decided to "mingle storm and tempest over boundless earth." Everything and everyone would be destroyed by a great flood except Deucalion, son of the god Prometheus, and his wife Pyrrha, who was the goddess Pandora's daughter. Warned by Prometheus, the two humans survived

"And now, as in Greek mythology, this Hebrew Jupiter decides to drown everything he has made save Noah and his crew. How he is going to drown the fish we are not told. To them a flood would be a red-letter day."

Lloyd Graham, *Deceptions and Myths of the Bible*

"Entire shoals of fossil fish over large areas, numbering billions of specimens, are found in a state of agony, but with no mark of a scavenger's attack."

Immanual Velikovsky, *Earth in Upheaval*

the nine-day storm in a great wooden chest built by Deucalion. This finally landed on Mount Parnassus in Greece.

In the ancient Chinese encyclopedia, with 4,320 volumes believed to contain all knowledge up to that time, references were made to a flood hero by the name of Fo-Hsi. Fo-Hsi, his wife, and their three children escaped the Deluge and started the world again.

Other Chinese traditions say all Chinese descend from Nu-Wah, an ancient survivor of a great flood. Dr. E.W. Thwing, a researcher who lived in China for many years, studied Chinese writing trying to discover whether "Nu-wah" was the same person as Noah. Although he couldn't conclude both were the same person, he did discover that the Chinese word for "ship" is a character made up of the picture of a "boat" and "eight mouths." According to Thwing, this means the first ship was a boat carrying eight people.

The Flood in the Koran

The Koran, the holy book of Islam, also describes a flood. Muslims believe this book is a transcript of a tablet kept in heaven and revealed by the Angel Gabriel to the Prophet Mohammed in A.D. 610.

In chapter 71 of the Koran, the Koran states: "We sent forth Noah to his people, saying 'Give warning to your people before a woeful scourge overtakes them.'" Noah warned the people to serve Allah, in which case they would be forgiven their wrongdoings, which included worshipping many idols. But the people would not listen. "Each time I call to them to seek your pardon," Noah states, "they thrust their fingers in their ears and draw their cloaks over their heads, persisting in sin and bearing themselves with insolent pride."

Because of the people's wrongdoing, "they were overwhelmed by the Flood and cast into the Fire. They found none to help them besides Allah." The faithful were forgiven, but all unbelievers were destroyed.

These stories are representative of the hundreds of flood tales from the world's cultures. There seem to be a few major items common to most of them.

First, humanity somehow displeased God or the gods. Usually this resulted from immoral living habits or disrespect for religion. Second, one person is warned of the impending doom. This person is able to save at least one family member or friend, but everyone else is destroyed by the Flood.

Finally, animals are part of the Flood story in some way. They may convey the Flood warning, accompany people to the sailing vessel or mountain, or be used to test for land.

Historians do not know why similar flood tales exist in such different cultures. It is possible there were many local floods and each culture had a story to explain the flood and why some people survived and others did not. Historian James Frazer does not see any relation to a single divine original, such as the biblical Flood of Genesis. Nor can any of them, according to Frazer, be traced to a Babylonian origin. However, archaeologist G.S. Wegener feels that all the legends must have had some starting point, perhaps one in common.

The three general areas of disagreement among the various flood stories include:
• The type of boat. Boats mentioned include canoes, a box, wooden jug, rafts, and, of course, the Ark. Some stories also talk about mountains, islands, or underground caves as shelter instead of boats.
• The number of people saved differs. The usual range is from two to eight, but in some stories only one person has been saved, while in a few stories, hundreds are.
• The final rescue site differs. Since legends come from all over the world, sites include Mount Ararat in Turkey, Mount Parnassus in Greece, the Himalayas in India, Keddie Peak in California, and Mouna-Kea in Hawaii.

"It is easy to see how the legend could grow, a few drowned hamlets becoming in retrospect populous cities and their surrounding fields being enlarged into an entire kingdom."
Encyclopedia of World Mythology

"We need not claim that the biblical accounts in Genesis are easy to understand, but at least we should give these ancient writers the courtesy of being taken seriously."
Robert Brow, *Christianity Today*

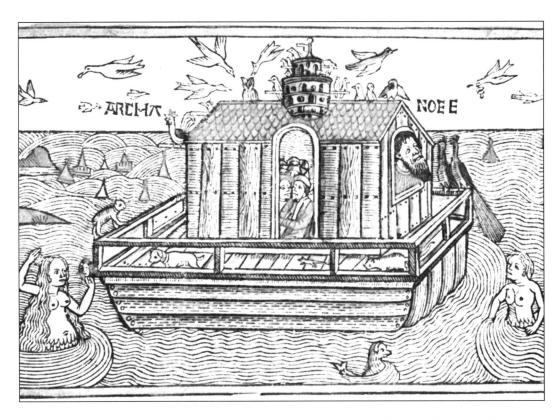

Noah looks for the return of the dove. From a fifteenth-century German Bible.

Is there a common origin to all the stories, with details changing in the passage, as Wegener says? Or, as Frazer maintains, is there no relation between any of the stories, and the different items in them mere coincidence?

The differing evidence suggests three possible conclusions: First, there was one universal Flood, but as the story passed along from generation to generation, and as populations moved from one part of the world to another, people turned the story into a local happening. "There is ample evidence," author Charles Berlitz writes, "that there was a common memory of a phenomenon that affected all areas of the planet and was therefore remembered by tribes and nations that did not know of each others' existence and reported their own experiences in local context."

A second possible conclusion is that there were many major floods, each with its own story. Because people were unaware of neighboring countries or tribes, they presumed their flood was a flood of the entire world. "On the whole, then," writes Frazer, "there seems to be good reason for thinking that some and probably many diluvial flood traditions are merely exaggerated reports of floods which actually occurred, whether as the result of heavy rain, earthquake waves, or other causes."

The third possibility is that there was a universal Flood followed by other minor, local floods, and the stories became confused. "Any destructive flood leaves behind telltale signs in the Earth's crust," writes author Charles Balsiger. "But in what form are these signs after 5,000 years? Will we be able to recognize them as results of a Deluge?"

That disastrous floods occur all over the world, and have done so for thousands of years, is not doubted. However, geological proof that Noah's Flood was the parent of them all continues to be controversial.

Three

Is There Geologic Evidence of the Flood?

In the 1980s, a branch of scholarly research called *creationism* became popular among those who believe that Noah's Flood happened just as it is described in the book of Genesis. These scholars are known as *creationists*. They seek evidence for their position that there was one universal Flood sent by God, and that Noah did indeed build an Ark. Creationists believe that they can prove the events of the great Flood by examining the geologic record, just as geologists study the earth's surface to learn about other past events.

There is great disagreement between creationists and geologists as to the earth's age. Creationists state that according to the book of Genesis, the earth is approximately 6,000 years old. Humans and animals came into being at that time, only to be destroyed by a worldwide flood, and then renewed. This Flood took place approximately 4,300 years ago.

This viewpoint is in marked contrast to the most widely accepted geologic evidence that the Earth was formed about 4.5 billion years ago. Geologists say that fossils, rock formations, and other evidence prove the earth is ancient. In their research,

Mt. Ararat is a foreboding place, with treacherous slopes and frequent bad weather that makes searching for the Ark difficult.

gists have not found any satisfactory evidence that there ever was a single Flood.

The creationist view, however, asserts ample evidence for a universal Flood. Only this type of disaster, they argue, could have caused geological features such as mountains, canyons, oceans, rivers, and other great earth features in the 6,000 years since the world began.

What natural events could cause a worldwide Flood? David Balsiger, author of *In Search of Noah's Ark*, states that Earth's atmosphere before the Flood contained a great amount of water vapor, making Earth humid, somewhat like a greenhouse. Instead of rain, heavy dew kept the plants watered. A constant, heavy dew covered everything. The atmosphere was like a canopy of water vapor covering the earth.

About 4,300 years ago, Balsiger says, a meteorite collision may have caused disruptions in the earth's atmosphere. He bases this on a statement in the

The Deluge supposedly destroyed every living thing on Earth. Could the waters of heaven and earth ever be enough to drown the entire earth?

Encyclopedia Britannica which says "the number of meteorites falling in the centuries before Christ was higher than today." He also cites geologic data of damage done by great meteorites of the past. "There is little need to speculate on what such an impact would do to the Earth in biblical times," Balsiger says. "It would start an indescribable series of events that could easily have sparked the Flood."

In Balsiger's view, the meteorite collision may have caused the water vapor canopy to collapse, and its water to dump onto the earth all at once. This could have produced oceanic tidal waves and giant upheavals in the sea floor. The earth and all its people would have been flooded.

What Is the Evidence?

As proof of ocean flood waters rising high enough to cover mountain tops, Balsiger cites Lake Urmia, in Iran, which is over 4,000 feet above sea level. Lake Urmia has no connection to an ocean and is completely surrounded by high mountains, yet its salt concentration is high—23 percent.

Another unusual site is Lake Van, in eastern Turkey, which is over 5,000 feet above sea level. It has no connection to the ocean, but contains salt water and salt-water herring. There are also cube-shaped salt clusters, as big as grapefruit, which have been found on Mount Ararat 7,000 feet high.

Geologists do not doubt that at one time the ocean was thousands of feet higher than it is today. However, this was billions of years ago, they state. As the waters dried up, small inland seas were left. As these inland seas dried up, the salt in them thickened. This, according to geologists, explains salt found on mountains and in the waters of high mountain lakes. However, no scientist can accurately date the age of a salt grain, so we still do not know precisely when the salt on Ararat and other mountains originated. Was the ocean level naturally high billions of years ago, or did a flood 4,300 years ago cause the ocean to rise to extreme heights? The debates continue as scientists and creationists look for more evidence to solve the mystery. And, indeed, creationists say they do have more evidence.

What appear to be the ruins of sunken cities still lie on the bottom of the Mediterranean Sea, off the African Coast, in the Carribean, and elsewhere.

In addition, pillow lava is found on Mount Ararat at 14,000 feet above sea level. Pillow lava is formed when lava pours into water, then is rapidly chilled so that circular formations resembling pillows develop. Finding pillow lava on Ararat implies that lava poured out from Ararat while it was under water. Genesis 7:20 states the Flood covered even the highest mountains with fifteen cubits of water (approxi-

The rivers of the Middle East, Asia, and Africa—the Biblical world—frequently rise and flood the surrounding farmlands and villages. Was the Flood merely a local disaster?

mately twenty-five feet). Finding pillow lava on Ararat could be proof, according to author Balsiger, that flood waters reached at least 14,000 feet high. Again, geologists do not dispute these observations. However, instead of flood action, they say earthquakes are a possible cause. The movements of the continents can lift enormous rock masses thousands of feet, causing rock layers to buckle, fold, and overturn. This could cause the flooding of coastal cities, the movement of beach soil inland, and the isolation of salt-water lakes on mountain tops.

How Long Ago?

Some scientists believe that any catastrophic floods which occurred were strictly local. An example cited by author Balsiger is the flood layer Sir Leonard Woolley uncovered at the Ur excavations. Local floods might have been caused by tidal waves, volcanic action, heavy rain, local earthquake, or rivers rising. This is called the "local flood theory."

Scientists generally agree there was a great catastrophe throughout the world more than 65 million years ago. Prior to this, geologists state, the world was much warmer than it is now. It had a steamy tropical climate with huge plants and lots of rain. The earth had only one great land mass rather than several continents separated by water as it has now. On this relatively flat land dinosaurs moved about with ease, despite their size. Then they died out. So did 70 percent of all other life on earth.

What caused the catastrophe? Some geologists believe the world got too hot, others state it developed hot and cold seasons, and a third group says it got too cold. A fourth theory blames increased rainfall, while a fifth theory mentions decreased rainfall. Creationists claim a universal Flood occurring 4,300 years ago—not 65 million years ago—was the cause, exactly as described in the Bible. There is a great deal of time difference between 65 million

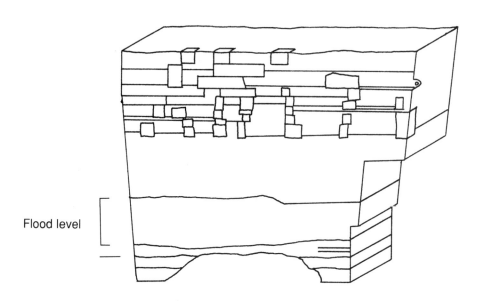

Flood level

Sir Leonard Woolley's discovery of a mud layer covering the city of Ur in Mesopotamia was cited as evidence that the story of the Flood was true.

years and 4,300 years. Both creationists and geologists claim they have more than adequate proof for their dating of the world and any catastrophe that changed its face. Among the proofs are fossils found in pits, rocks, and on top of mountains. But dating these fossils is another cause of controversy.

What Is the Fossil Evidence?

Fossils are the remains or traces of dead animals and plants that have been preserved over the ages. Fossils are very rarely formed because most living things decompose (rot), or are otherwise destroyed by scavengers or natural accidents after they die. But in some cases, the plant or animal is quickly buried in water-carried sediment and thus preserved. In many cases, fossils are quite well-preserved, looking

Fossils, such as this angel fish, are really impressions in stone that reveal the appearance of animals and plant life that died long ago. Creationists and geologists disagree over the age of fossils and what significance they have to various flood theories.

much like they did while alive. Some fossils are thousands, even millions of years old, according to geologists, and some are much younger. Fossils can give many clues to the era they came from.

In A.D. 1669, English scientist Robert Hook stated that all fossils were the remains of animals who died in the Great Flood. Even today, creationists list many locations of group fossils that seem to support this idea.

In Santa Barbara, California, a United States Geological Survey report mentions a petrified "fish bed" with "more than a billion fish" in it. *Petrified* means organic matter that has been changed into a stony substance. This only happens after thousands of years. How did all those fish get trapped in mud? Did a flood carry them along and drop them all at once, along with tons of dirt?

Another strange sedimentary deposit is found near Diamondville, Wyoming. It contains many large fossil fish and plants. The deposit includes alligators, sunfish, deep sea bass, turtles, sea shells, and animal remains—a collection not normally found together.

Geisenthal, Germany, has a rock bed containing more than 6,000 animal remains in addition to those of insects, sea shells, and plants. These are so well preserved that even bits of hair, feathers and scales remain. If not by a single catastrophic Flood, how did all these animals come together?

Fossil fishes have also been found on mountain tops. Whale skeletons have been found in the Himalayas, the world's highest mountain range. Fish bones and clam shells have been found on mountain peaks. Seashells have been found on Mt. Ararat at 10,000 feet. Creationists say all this fossil evidence is proof of a universal Flood.

Geologists, however, say there are other explanations for fossils finds such as these. In the 1800s, author Charles Darwin showed how animals from prehistoric times were the ancestors of animals we see today. Animals and plants in one form or another have been around for some 590 million years, Darwin said—and most modern scientists agree.

Scientists can prove the age of certain plants and animals by dating fossils. One method used is *radiometric dating*. Radiometric dating measures the loss or decay of various elements in matter, such as Potassium-argo, Rubidium-strontium, and Uranium-thorium-lead. The presence or absence of these compounds in a fossil can determine how old it is. Scientists say radiometric dating can track back over 100 million years.

In addition, scientists are able to analyze the various layers of the earth. They have not found one large layer that is present all over the earth, as would be expected if there were one large flood. Instead, the earth has many layers, different from region to region, each containing unique fossils. The deepest layers everywhere, and therefore the oldest, hold the stony remains of trilobites. The uppermost, or newest layers, contain fossils quite similar to modern species. The geologic evidence suggests that the oldest fossil layers are about 440 million years old.

The sedimentary beds in California, Wyoming, Germany and other sites, cited by creationists as probable proof of a universal Flood, were most likely caused by massive local flooding, according to geologists and other scientists.

The fossils found on any continent tend to be closely related to animals who lived on that continent, rather than animals living on other continents. Any universal flood would have carried sediment throughout the world, so scientists could expect to find fossils of animals that lived on other continents. It would be like finding a kangaroo fossil in China or mammoth elephant skeleton in Australia, but this sort of species mixture has never been found.

"If creationism were correct, a continent's extinct animals wouldn't necessarily resemble its modern ones, unless God had specifically arranged the fossils in the earth to trick us into accepting evolution."

Professor T.G. Bonney, *Science and the Flood*

"This neatly packaged system of geologic interpretation has the effect of making it practically impossible ever to dislodge it by any amount of evidence."

John Whitcomb and Henry Morris, *The Genesis Flood*

Skeptics of the Flood story state that Noah and his family could never crowd two of every animal onto the Ark, no matter how big.

Theologian John C. Whitcomb and hydraulic engineer Henry M. Morris are two founders of the modern creationist movement. They disagree with most scientific analysis of the earth's layers.

They state that tremendous upheavals wracked the earth at the same time as the Great Flood (earthquake, volcanic activity, and tidal waves) and disrupted the normal processes of nature. Therefore, modern analysis of sedimentary layers would not be accurate for this period, they say. For creationists, the fossil record (meaning fossil imprints in rock that indicate life existed millions of years ago) is not a record at all. It is a jumbled arrangement of bones from all creatures that died in the Flood.

Geological fossil dating, while increasingly sophisticated, is by geologists' own admission not totally accurate. It is possible that new techniques will prove current dating to be accurate, or indicate ideas that need to be corrected. Creationists, too, admit their dating techniques are not perfect. Their analysis of the Bible is done by humans, and while the Bible is believed by millions to be infallible, humans are not. While conflicting viewpoints are plentiful, it is possible that in the future, additional discoveries will shed brighter light on the fossil record—and Noah's Flood.

Four

Could Noah Build An Ark?

We cannot go back in time with a movie camera, and prove that Noah built an ark. Instead, we must examine the biblical Ark information, plus interpretations from scholars and scientists. Then we must attempt to separate fact from fancy. First, let us look at the biblical description of the Ark: "Make thee an ark of gopher wood; with rooms shalt thou make the ark, and shalt pitch it within and without with pitch. And this is how thou shalt make it: the length of the ark three hundred cubits, the breadth of it thirty cubits. A light shalt thou make to the ark, and to a cubit shalt thou finish it upward; and the door of the ark shalt thou set in the side thereof; with lower, second, and third stories shalt thou make it."

Using these dimensions, scholars have tried to calculate how big the Ark would be, how large a cargo it could carry, even how heavy it was, and whether it could float at all.

According to author John Warwick Montgomery, the Ark's weight was 48,600,000 pounds when fully loaded with people, animals, food and supplies. This is based on its *displacement tonnage* (the weight of sea water displaced by a ship when submerged).

Opposite page: "And the dove came back to him in the evening, and lo, in her mouth a freshly plucked olive leaf; so Noah knew that the waters had subsided from the earth." (Gen. 8:11)

"If God was able to create the entire world, and the sun, moon, stars and planets, plus entire galaxies in space beyond our imagination, could God then not feed animals and people in a large boat for 150 days?"

Mark Peterson, *Noah and the Flood*

"There simply could not have been an Ark as described in the Bible. It would have had to accommodate 3,858,920 animals. If the dimensions of the craft as laid out in Genesis are accepted, that is a snug one-quarter cubic foot per beast."

Robert Moore, quoted in *Maclean's* magazine

Montgomery figured the displacement from the dimensions given in the Bible.

According to author David Balsiger, it would take 280,000 cubic feet of timber, or between 9,000 and 13,000 planks, to construct the boat. Some of the planks could have been twelve inches thick.

The Bible says "resinwood," or more commonly, "gofer" or "gopher wood," was used. No modern wood is known by that name. A few scholars think gopher wood is oleander or cypress. Others argue the wood was cedar. They claim oleander is too bushy for boat use, and cypress and cedar are mentioned by their modern names elsewhere in the Bible. Most scholars now believe white oak was used to build the Ark.

White oak was widely used for shipbuilding at the time. Richard Bliss, professor of science at the University of Wisconsin, has several reasons for believing white oak might have been used to construct the Ark. First, there was lots of it growing in the Middle East. Second, it was free—all Noah had to do was chop it and use it. Third, it is almost indestructible. White oak is extremely waterproof and hard. Finally, it splits easily when cut, so it is useful for construction.

In the more than 100 years of Ark construction, other kinds of wood would have dried or decayed before the job was finished. "But white oak, as it drys," Bliss says, "becomes more compact, making it even more waterproof and highly desirable."

According to Dr. Frederick Filby, a noted Biblical researcher, a mineral pitch, or tarry substance, was used to seal Ark joints against water and moisture. Ample amounts of pitch are found in the Babylonian area where the Ark was constructed. Thus Bliss and Filby agree it would have been possible to build the Ark with the materials available in Noah's time.

There were no power saws and power drills in Biblical times. What tools might Noah have used to complete a big boat project? According to the Bible, Tubal-Cain, believed by some to be Noah's brother-in-law, was able to forge bronze and iron. If this is true, perhaps metal tools were available prior to the Flood.

If metal tools were not available, could Noah have accomplished his goal with more primitive equipment? Archaeologists have proved that the pharaohs of Egypt built the Great Pyramid using similar primitive tools. The Great Pyramid has two million stone blocks weighing 5,000 pounds a piece. And it was built with such skill that each of its 756-foot sides are almost exactly alike. What the

The Ark of Noah supposedly took 100 years to build and its dimensions were specified by God.

pharoahs could accomplish, says Balsiger, Noah aided by God could certainly do.

What Did the Ark Look Like?

The Ark story is the first instance in the Bible where dimensions and descriptions are given. It is estimated that Noah's Ark was taller than a three-story building and half the length of a football field, although exact dimensions vary from scholar to scholar. Most commonly the Ark is thought to have been about 450 feet wide and 45 feet high.

According to models and drawings done from the Biblical description, such as those done by the seventeenth-century Jesuit Athanasius Kircher, the Ark had a flat bottom, was rectangular in shape and had straight sides. According to Balsiger, it was large enough to carry more cargo than 569 railway freight cars! It could have carried more than 30,000 animals and birds of varying sizes. In his view, the Ark's

Merchant seaman and ark hunter David Fasold believes the Ark was not made from wood at all, but from reeds.

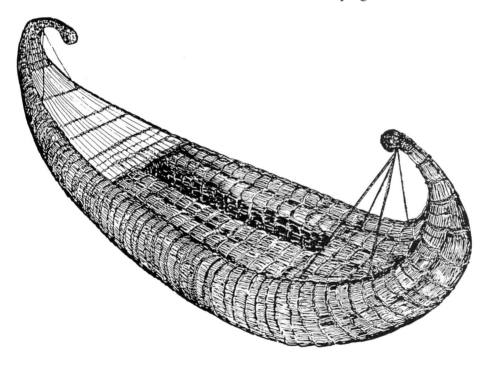

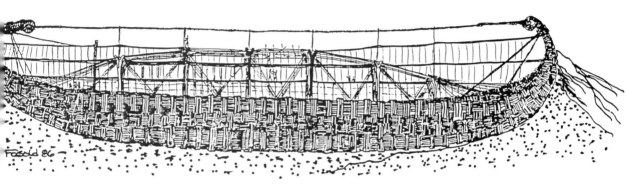

three decks were about 14 feet high, with the space between them another 15 feet. Two long dividing walls along the ship's length made a central passage. Along either side of the passage were more divisions, marking off compartments, rooms or cabins, depending on the use. Each room had a door, in addition to the main Ark door. There would also be a ramp for the animals and stairs for Noah and his family.

The Bible mentions the Ark having both light and air. Since glass was not made at the time, light had to come through an opening. According to Dr. Frederick Filby, the "window" was possibly an open space just below the roof along the length of both sides. It would be covered by an overhang to keep out the rain, with some type of sliding wooden panels as a weather barrier.

Another researcher, David Fasold, concluded that

Another view of the ship as Fasold imagines it must have been to be seaworthy, and to hold the necessary cargo.

> "Noah and his sons clearly couldn't house, feed and tend this menagerie. Sadly, creation scientists watched the overloaded ark sink under its own weight."
>
> Jared Diamond, *Discover* magazine

> "In every way, therefore, the Ark as designed was highly stable, admirably suited for its purpose of riding out the storms of the year of the great Flood."
>
> J.W. Montgomery, *The Quest for Noah's Ark*

a wooden ship of such size could never be seaworthy, and that Noah's Ark was actually constructed from bound reeds—like a giant, enclosed raft. He bases his theory in part on what he calls the mistranslation of "gopher wood." If the Ark were made from lighter materials, this would certainly have simplified its construction.

Would the Ark Float?

Authors Balsiger and Montgomery, however, claim the wooden Ark was built for stability. It wasn't designed to go anyplace speedily, like a motor boat. It had no tiller, no rudder, not even oars. Instead it floated through the Flood, like a cork, travelling 900 miles from Babylonia to reach Mount Ararat in the biblical 150 days.

Genesis says the Deluge floodwaters rose at least fifteen cubits, or at least twenty-two feet, above the highest mountains. This would give the Ark, according to Whitcomb and Balsinger, ample room to float. The Ark was sturdy, too, according to geologist Henry Morris. Even heavy waves and strong winds would not have tipped it over.

Many attempts have been made to duplicate the Ark—full size, smaller, and in miniature—to see whether the translated biblical design was functional. In 1604 a Dutch merchant named Peter Jansen had a boat built with exactly the same proportions as the biblical Ark, but smaller: 120 feet long, 20 feet high and 12 feet wide. It proved quite capable of carrying freight.

The first known ship longer than Noah's Ark was built in 1884. It was the *Eturia*, a Cunard ocean liner. Lacking adequate equipment, modern people had not tackled a boat of this size before. This led Canadian biblical researcher Arthur C. Custance to state there may have been an Ark, but it couldn't have been nearly as big as the Bible said. Perhaps scholars misunderstood the dimension "cubit" as used in Genesis.

An Ark model was also made by Balsiger and Charles Sellier. They had it tested by an "independent laboratory." The results, according to the unidentified lab were: The Ark, as described in the Bible, could have survived 200-foot-high waves without capsizing unless it was hit broadside. "But the surprising thing revealed by the tests," Balsiger and Sellier mention, "was that the Ark naturally propelled its bow into the waves. It's a remarkably stable vessel."

In 1968, Meir Ben-Uri of Israel, a leading synagogue designer and Biblical scholar, designed an ark following his own interpretation of Biblical dimensions. The design, according to Ben-Uri, was like a long rectangle, a shape easily accommodating three decks and space for at least 2,000 animals—far fewer then the claims of Balsiger.

Such a vessel could have been built while lying at an angle on one side, Ben-Uri calculates. Animals could climb easily into the Ark via a ramp and enter through the door. As the Ark began floating, it would, by design, right itself. The "door" would tilt and become a "skylight", therefore conforming to biblical specifications. Water could not enter the Ark from its sides. It would have been a seaworthy and practical vessel.

How Did the Animals Get to Noah's Ark?

One of the most hotly debated parts of the Noah's Ark controversy concerns the Ark animals. In Genesis, Noah was told to bring two of every living creature into the Ark: "And of every living thing of all flesh, two of every sort shalt thou bring into the ark, to keep them alive with thee; they shall be male and female. Of the fowl after their kind, and of the cattle after their kind, of every creeping thing of the ground after its kind, two of every sort shall come unto thee, to keep them alive. And take thou unto thee of all food that is eaten, and gather it to thee."

Columnist Robert Yoakum and others scoff at this

task. Could Noah have brought every living species aboard the Ark? "I'll betcha it would take three guys a hundred years to round up a million animals by twos. Sometimes it takes me a couple of hours just to find my dog or catch the cat," wrote Yoakum.

Was it possible, without trains, planes, cars, or any other convenient transportation to gather all the animals requested on the Ark? "The sloths and armadillos, little fitted by nature for long journeys," wrote geologist Hugh Miller, "would have required to be ferried across the Atlantic."

Biblical analysts disagree with this. Noah was not told to "gather" the animals. They were to "come" to him, that is, come of their own accord. How did they know how to do this? Perhaps by direction from God, perhaps instinct. Animals do have phenomenal instincts—migratory flights in fall, homing instincts, food-finding capabilities—all of which still mystify humanity but are nevertheless fact.

Inside the Ark

Some of the hypothetical descriptions of life on the Ark are quite detailed. Athanasius Kircher (1602-1680) a German Jesuit priest and the first of the noted creationists, spent many hours analyzing the needs of the Ark and figuring out a precise layout. He calculated there were three decks, each with about 300 stalls, some big enough to hold elephants. The top deck, or *Ornithotropheion*, would have contained the birds plus Noah and his family. The middle deck, or *Bromatodocheion*, would have held supplies. The Lower Deck, or *Zootropheion*, would have held the rest of the animals.

For all the animals to survive, there had to be food. For the meat eaters there would have been smoked meat and chickens; for grass eaters, grain and hay; seeds and berries for the birds; straw for the animals to sleep on; and plenty of water for all to drink.

Noah, his wife, his sons, and their wives might

Kircher's elaborate deck plans show every compartment on the gigantic ship where the animals and stores might have gone.

DECK ONE

Eagle, French, Eared Owls · Empty Room
Exotic Birds · Birds of Paradise
Warblers · Quail
Notes, Crows, Coots · Swallows
Warblers & Wagtails ·
Ducks, Various Species · Cuckoos
Domestic & Wild Geese · Chickadees
· Sparrows
Herons · Ravens
Cranes, Storks · Japheth's Room
· Ham's Room
Ostriches · Shem's Room
Falcons, Various Species · Noah's Room
· Dining Room
Eagles, Various Species · Kitchen
Vultures · Larder
Hawks · Singing Birds, Nightingales, Larks & Chaffinches
Heron & Pelican Species · Fowl, Various Species
Peacocks · Pigeons, Doves, Turtle Doves
Parrots ·
Magpies · Gyrfalcons & Harpies
Kingfishers · Exotic Birds such as Kingbirds, Crakes, Shrikes, Titmice & Wrynecks
Budgies ·
Pheasants, Grouse ·
Ptarmick, Umbrells ·
Ventilators · Stairways

DECK TWO

Empty Storeroom · Cattle, Horses & Asses
Straw for animals · Hay for Herbivores
Grain for animals · Winter Fodder
Water Casks
Oats · Lentils, Rice
Barley · Beans, Peas
Winter Wheat · Chestnuts
Wheat · Nuts, Acorns
Sheep · Pigeons
Cheese · Butter
Goats · Chickens
Bread, Smoked Meat · Dried Fish & Candles, Honey
Pears, Apples · Salt, Metal, Minerals
Seeds, Berries ·
Spices · Olive Oil
Firewood · Hand Mills, Oven
Ropes · Iron Tools
Empty Room · Cloth, Utensils
Mechanical Tools for the Future World · Agricultural Implements
BROMATODOCHEON

DECK THREE

Cistern · Storeroom
· Badgers
Boars, Pigs · Porcupines
Foxes · Tortoises
Wolves · Seals
Lynxes · Indian Pigs
Unicorns · Maltese
Panthers · Purebreeds
Tigers · Greyhounds
· Retrievers
Bears · Chamois
Lions · Reindeer
Rhinos · Deer
Elephants · Cattle
Camels · Goats
Dromedaries · Sheep
Horses · Bison
Asses · Elk
Onagers · Gazelles
Cats · Buckbucks
Monkeys · Hippos
Rabbits · Crocodiles
Squirrels · Otters
Indian Pigs · Beavers
Cones · Cistern
Empty Room ·
ZOOTROPHEION

Athanasius Kircher, a German Jesuit from the seventh century, used the description in Genesis to imagine the size and shape of the Ark.

share a kitchen and dining room, but would have separate bedrooms. Their food might include bread, butter, oats, and barley, plus whatever else might be needed for a very long voyage, since Noah was not told how long the Flood would last.

Kircher's drawings also allowed space for equipment Noah would need both on the Ark and after it landed, including rope, tools, cloth and candles. Kircher claimed there would be room for 130 mammals, 150 bird types, and 30 different kinds of snakes on board the Ark. He did not think fish or other water creatures needed an Ark to survive a flood, so he did not put these on board.

Clearly, different scholars are in wide disagreement over how big the Ark was, and how much it could carry. Author Robert Moore pointed out that if Kircher's floor plan was correct, there was no way Noah could have saved enough animals. According to his calculations, Noah would have had to bring 3,858,920 animals on board in order to have the species we have today, an impossible number for the size of Noah's boat.

Zoologist Ernst Mayre wrote that his calculations showed the Ark might have carried 3,700 mammals, 8,600 birds, 6,300 reptiles, 2,500 amphibians, in addition to sponges, worms, and other creatures, or a total of 1,072,300 animals, again a figure far too high for the size of the craft.

Creationist authors Tim LaHaye and John Morris estimate Noah only had to house between 35,000 and 50,000 animals. Nor, they say, were animals the same size as they are now. According to LaHaye and Morris, they were much smaller, about the size of sheep. Thus there was ample room on board the Ark.

LaHaye and Morris's statistics show the Ark was equal in size to 569 railroad cars. "Since 240 animals the size of a sheep could be housed in a standard two-deck stock car," they write, "by dividing the total number of animals on the Ark by 240...we

"I think anyone who tries to visualize the construction of a vessel 450 feet long by four men will realize that the size of the timbers alone for a 'building' 45 feet high (analogous to a four-story apartment building) would seem by their sheer massiveness to be beyond the powers of four men to handle."

Arthur Custance, *The Extent of the Flood*

"Some may feel the Ark was too large for early man to have attempted. A survey of the ancient world shows in fact the very reverse. One is constantly amazed at the enormous tasks which our ancestors attempted."

J.W. Montgomery, *The Quest for Noah's Ark*

A "drogue" stone, one of twelve discovered by ark hunter David Fasold on Mt. Ararat. The stone was supposedly tethered to the Ark with a rope through the hole at the top, working like an anchor.

find the Ark was not too small for the task." In other words, the animals occupied only 36 percent of it.

Were Any Animals Left Out?

What happened to all the fish and bugs and oysters? According to British scientist Arthur Jones there's nothing in the biblical text requiring Noah to take these on board. Fish swim, oysters live in water, and many bugs can live on a tiny floating scrap. Therefore, these creatures would have survived the Flood without Noah's help. Skeptics respond to this by saying a universal Flood would have mixed salt and fresh water. The fish and other water creatures would die because they live in only one or the other. Creationists state that while billions of fish might have died from the water mix, enough would have survived to reproduce.

What happened to the animals that did not make it on board the Ark? They, perhaps, became extinct. We do know of many extinct species, such as dinosaurs.

Whether a huge Ark was possible to build in more primitive times is still a subject for debate. It would have been an enormous amount of work for Noah, even if his family helped. And could the Ark have held all those animals? Morris, LaHaye, Balsiger and Montgomery are certain the Ark would have been adequate in size to hold its cargo and that it would have been quite sea-worthy. Others, such as physiologist Jared Diamond, state the Ark would have sunk under the weight of all the animals and supplies. But suppose it was seaworthy, and did float easily to Mount Ararat. Might it still be there?

Five

Does the Ark Exist?

Scholars and scientists from a number of fields have debated the possibility of Noah's Ark for over 1,500 years.

Some people claim that the Ark has been preserved by ice and snow for 5,000 years in an unreachable ravine near the top of Mount Ararat, a 16,946-foot-high peak in Eastern Turkey. Mount Ararat, also called *Agri Dagh* or "Mountain of Pain," has snow all year round and severe blizzards that happen often and unexpectedly. This peak is one of the most inhospitable and hazardous areas in the world. But if the Ark is there, in its entirety or in fragments, it is a prize indeed. Searchers have braved Agri Dagh for centuries trying to find it.

It is easy for skeptics to say the Ark no longer exists in any form, on Ararat or any other mountain. Proof does seem elusive, yet scholars, who should be the first to scoff, are among the mountain's earliest climbers. They were driven by one thought—that at any step the Ark could be right beneath their feet.

One of the first stories about an Ark seeker concerns Jacob, a Mesopotamian bishop, climbing in about A.D. 325. In his prayers he asked God's per-

mission to find the Holy Ark. Hour after hour he climbed through the snow. Then, thirsty and tired, he lay down for a brief rest. Upon awakening, he discovered a spring had miraculously appeared near his sleeping spot. ("Jacob's Well" still remains as a mountain landmark.)

Jacob continued his climb. But after each nap he would awake to find himself down at the bottom of the mountain again. Finally an angel appeared, saying Jacob had been carried down by angels because "The Ark is forbidden territory to man, until God chooses to reveal it."

For a long time, everyone believed Ararat was unclimbable. But in 1829 a German-Russian professor, Dr. Friedrich Parrot, proved the skeptics wrong. Ignoring local taboos that said God would severely punish people trying to climb to the Ark, Parrot became the first man to reach the summit, the supposed Ark site.

The last day of his journey began at dawn. "At first dawn we roused ourselves up," Parrot wrote. "The last tracts of rocky fragments were crossed... and we once more trod on the limits of perpetual

This 1960 expedition, with Turkish troop escort, believed they had found the Ark buried in this spot. The curvature of the land mimics the shape of a hull.

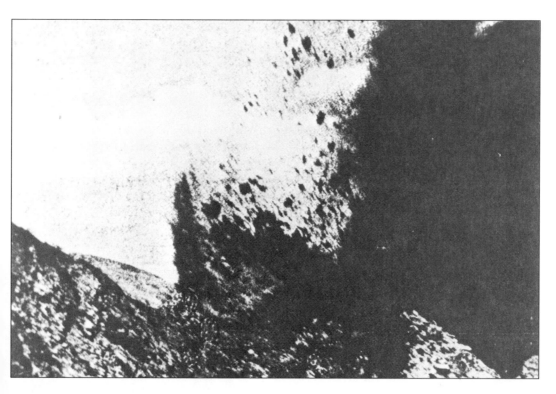

snow." Cutting steps in the ice, Parrot and his companions proceeded laboriously up the mountain, finally reaching the top. Though the Ark was not seen, Parrot wrote, "It is obvious that on the top of Ararat might easily be a sufficient depth of ice to cover the Ark, which was only about 100 feet high." Ice and snow on tall mountains can easily be as much as 100 feet thick.

After Parrot's expedition, many persons raced to find the Ark. Some were motivated by thoughts of fame, others were adventurers seeking challenge. Some wanted to prove that the Ark, and therefore the story of the Flood, were absolutely true. And there were a few who sought to prove the Ark was not there, and perhaps never was there. Many of the stories they brought back have become an integral part of the Ark legend.

Dynamite was used by the searchers to try and recover wood from beneath the soil. Wood fragments were reportedly found.

Mountain climbing is not to be taken lightly, so expeditions often use pack animals to carry supplies. Still, the harsh terrain and weather of Mt. Ararat has forced many searchers to turn back without success.

A Russian colonel named Khodzko, accompanied by sixty soldiers, climbed to Ararat's peak in 1850. On his way up, he encountered several electrical storms, as if Ararat was trying to discourage him from seeking its treasure. "2:30 p.m.—the wind increased in violence, and, to add to the difficulties, a dense fog swallowed up the peak," he wrote in his journal. The fury of the wind never ceased. "10 p.m. —a violent electrical storm began. The electricity did not zigzag across the air in the usual manner, but filled the place with blinding green, red, and white flashes." Whether the storm hid the Ark, or whether Colonel Khodzko never came near it, the Ark was not seen.

Six years later, a British war veteran, Major Robert Stuart, defied Kurdish guides (local villagers from around Ararat) who helped him get to a mere 6,000 feet on Ararat. "It is Holy ground," they said. "To proceed further would provoke heavenly wrath."

Stubbornly, with the Ark vision beckoning as the prize at the end of the climb, Stuart's group persisted. Some had to turn back later, but a few kept on, the Ark vision beckoning like some ghostly rainbow. A Major Fraser, part of Stuart's group, wrote: "When within a few hundred feet of the summit, I suddenly slipped and was shot downwards with the speed of lightening upwards of 1,000 feet; but instead of being dashed to pieces on the rocks a the foot of the glacier, some 4,000 feet below, I was stopped by the sprinkling of snow lying on the surface of the ice being pushed before me." Perhaps it was another

Ex-astronaut James Irwin with a Turkish army escort. Irwin believes the Ark is on Mt. Ararat, and has made several attempts to find it.

"No serious historian or archaeologist is interested in hunting for Noah's Ark."

Dr. Kirk Grayson, quoted in *Maclean's* magazine

"There will always be skeptics. There are people who don't believe we walked on the moon."

Astronaut and Ark hunter James Irwin, quoted in *Maclean's* magazine

way for Ararat to discourage visitors, but Stuart's determined group nevertheless climbed to the top. But they did not see any trace of the Ark.

Many climbers tackled Ararat in the following years, but few were as dedicated as John Libi, who made eight trips up the mountain between 1954 and 1969. The Ark site had beckoned to him in a dream, he stated. While on Ararat, he was chased by bears, caught pneumonia, and nearly died in a bad fall. On one expedition he was buried by snow up to his neck. Another time, rain washed his equipment and supplies down the mountain. On another attempt, a member of his group left camp and was never seen again. Libi made his last climb at age 73, this time actually reaching the place where he had dreamed the Ark rested. It was not there. He remained convinced that if he could keep looking, he would eventually find it. But because of his age, he did not go up again.

The failure of others before them to find the Ark or its fragments only seems to spur on new adventurers. Some of the descriptions of the hazards should have been enough to stop anybody, even the bravest. For example, John Morris wrote about his 1972 climb when lightening bolts struck suddenly at 13,000 feet. "Our hair was standing on end," he said. But that only slowed Morris down. It did not stop him, at least not at first. Then the lightening bolts knocked Morris and his men down a sharp rock-covered slope. Cleaning the blood off, they went painfully back down the mountain.

Photographer and mountaineer Ahmet Ali Arslan has stated that rock slides are a worse problem than the snow avalanches on Ararat. Volcanic rocks, he says—some of them as big as trucks—come speeding down at 120 miles per hour. And it s not just one rock, but thousands at a time. The slides can be started by something as simple as a wild goat jumping.

Arslan had climbed the mountain seventeen

In 1984 former U.S. astronaut James Irwin explored the southern face of Ararat in an attempt to locate Noah's Ark.

times by 1985, still without sighting the Ark. Even with all his experience, Ararat remains forbidding and dangerous. "It is a lone and very high mountain," Arslan says, "so it is like a giant lightening rod."

In addition, the cloud banks are so thick it is impossible for a climber to see where to put a metal climbing spike, a foot, or a hand. Accustomed to more solid conditions, the foolhardy try to keep going. However, snow and ice can form a crust that hides deep, dangerous holes. Sometimes the ice crust is partially melted. In the cloud bank, a climber can not see the softened crust. More than one adventurer has fallen through into the glacial deeps, never to be found.

The Climbs Continue

Climbers continue risking their lives, still certain the Ark is just out of sight. In 1982, Colonel James Irwin, an American astronaut who had walked on the moon, tried to climb Ararat's peak. Like others before him, the mountain seemed determined to discourage visitors. At 12,500 feet high, Irwin was struck on the head by a rock tumbling down the mountain. The force shoved him to a snowfield bottom, where he landed with five broken teeth, and many sprains and cuts. Trying to escape from the night cold, he crawled painfully into his sleeping bag. When he fell asleep, the bag, acting like a sled, slid down the steep mountain.

In the morning, rescuers found him. Irwin was taken by helicopter to a hospital. When he recovered, he went to Ararat two more times. He secured use of a Turkish army plane and made multiple flights around the mountain. Despite storms and fog, he took over 1,000 photographs at varying altitudes with special telephoto lenses.

Yet, when developed, only one photograph showed anything promising. Something that looked like a large piece of timber projected out of the ice.

Although Irwin did not climb Ararat again to investigate further, he said, "The Ark will be sought year after year. It's a mystery that will live on until it's rediscovered."

The modern political scene began interfering with the Ark search by 1985. In one instance, climbing groups from Japan, Germany, France and the U.S. started out to reach the top of Ararat. The Japanese climbers were halted and sent back by local rebels living in the mountains. The American group reached the 13,500-foot mark, then opened their tent flaps one morning to face the muzzle of a deadly Soviet AK-47. They were forced down the mountain in the bitter cold without their cold weather equipment, which had been taken away along with everything else.

Reaching another campsite they met the German and French expeditions, which had been treated the same way. "Go quick...back to America," was said by one of the raiders, who pointed down the mountain. This statement was followed by another, more muffled. But it sounded like, "Don't ever come back to our mountain."

Mount Ararat is only a few miles from the borders of Iran and Russia, both political hotspots. By 1974, the number of climbers became an increasing problem to Turkish officials. Both the Iranians and Soviets protested that some of those "climbers" might be spies, since Ararat looks down over their territories. To avoid an international incident, the Turkish government began limiting permits to climb the mountain, and even closed it down for a short time.

Then, in 1987, the Turkish central government again gave permission for limited searches. "But difficulties and opposition surfaced at every turn," writes Dr. John Morris, vice president at the Institute for Creation Research in California. Morris' group had hoped to mount an aerial search for the Ark. "It has been obvious for some time that ground-based

"A whole modern mythology has been built around the alleged 'evidence' provided by [Ark] expeditions— deathbed confessions that no one can check, hindsight identifications long after the event, aerial photographs showing anomalies that could be anything."

Magnus Magnusson, *Archaeology of the Bible*

"If the Ark is ever to be found, it will require the consistent, long-term planning of a Cape Kennedy operation, not the perspective of a Boy Scout outing."

J. W. Montgomery, *The Quest for Noah's Ark*

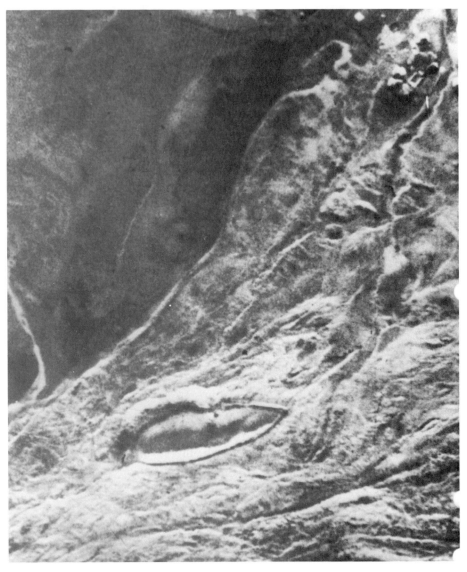

This photo was taken in 1959 by Turkish mapmakers flying over Ararat. The outline resembles the shape of a ship's hull, and the size of the feature is huge.

expeditions have very little chance of succeeding," Morris writes. Yet, despite careful plans and many permits, only one flight was eventually allowed by the local government. As if to protest even this one scientific excursion, Ararat that day had extremely cloudy weather.

Is it possible that the story about the angel who spoke to Jacob of Mesopotamia in A.D. 325 was correct in saying the Ark was forbidden territory, and would not be found until God chose to reveal it?

Are Searchers Looking In the Wrong Place?

Different versions of the Flood story claim different landing spots for the Ark. The Babylonian ark rested on Mount Nisir, the Hindu ark on Mount Himalaya, the Greek ark on Mount Parnassus, and the Moslem ark on Al Judi, which has sometimes been identified as Ararat and at other times as one of two other Middle Eastern mountains.

The Bible does not name a specific peak. It states "the *mountains* of Ararat." It is possible that Ararat may not refer to a single specific mountain but to a very large region once called Urartu, later called Armenia. This includes parts of modern Turkey, Iran, Iraq, and the Soviet Union. In this region there are hundreds of mountain peaks.

Is it possible that searchers have been risking their lives on the wrong mountain? Mount Ararat is the highest peak in this area. It stands utterly alone, rising sharply almost 17,000 feet from its base. The Armenians have always been completely certain the Ark landed here.

There are a few persons, such as Ark researcher and former merchant marine officer David Fasold, who believe the Ark rests on Mount Judi, about eighteen miles from Ararat. However, Charles Berlitz states, "It is the reported presence on Mount Ararat of the Ark of Noah that still holds the belief and imagination of many of the world's people."

"In many Turkish government offices, the whole search has become a joke. Many of the applicants have no credibility, no experience, no workable plan, have done no preparation, and seemingly have no reasonable chance for success. Many claim divine guidance and knowledge of the where-abouts of the ark."

John Morris, quoted in *Impact* magazine

"Does it make much difference, really, if the ark is found? By now it is immor-tal. If it did not find refuge in the heart of this mountain, it has found a safer refuge in the human heart. Here it has lived for thousands of years, and here it will live forever."

Gordon Gaskill, *Reader's Digest*

Six

Has Noah's Ark Ever Been Found?

Over the centuries many persons have reported retrieving segments of Ark wood, touching Ark wood, walking around an Ark visible through the ice, and even taking pictures of the Ark itself. Yet items that could be used to end the Ark debate have mysteriously disappeared.

Ancient Legends

Some of the earliest reported souvenirs of the Ark were reported by pilgrims from ancient times who climbed Ararat in search of the Ark. In 300 B.C., the historian Berossus mentioned Ararat climbers scraping pitch off the Ark and "using it for amulets," or good luck charms. None of the pitch reportedly found by pilgrims remains today. Considering Mount Ararat's harsh treatment of modern climbers, it is hard to believe the poorly-equipped pilgrims of the past could have succeeded in reaching the mountain top.

In 30 B.C., the biographer Nicolaus of Damascus stated the Ark's timbers were still on Ararat. Josephus, the historian, agreed with him 130 years later. But there's no record that either was ever on Ararat.

Opposite page: Fernand Navarra displays a piece of wood during a 1970 press conference in Los Angeles. Navarra claimed the wood was from Noah's Ark.

Ark hunters for several hundred years have climbed Mt. Ararat looking for the shape of a ship much like the one seen in this illustration.

Dutch adventurer Jan Struys, in 1670, told a daring tale of another Ark relic. Taken prisoner by bandits, he was given the chance to buy his freedom if he climbed Ararat and cured one of his captor's brothers. Struys reached the brother who was living as a monk on one of Ararat's slopes. The monk had a hernia. Struys, who had no medical background, managed to convince the monk that the hernia would be gone a few days after Struys departed. The grateful man gave his rescuer one of his few

prized possessions. "Take this," he said, handing over a small wooden cross. "It is carved from wood taken from Noah's Ark." The monk stated that he had gone into the sacred Ark, and, with his own hands, cut the wood fragment. Struys relic has been lost to time.

Haji Yearam

Ark searches are frought with more than physical adventure. Sometimes they are almost like psychological thrillers. Haji Yearam, an Armenian-born American, claimed to have seen the Ark itself. It is a strange tale he tells, stranger still because Yearam, who died in 1920 at the age of 82, dared tell it only shortly before his death.

As a youth, when living near Ararat, three men hired Yearam's father to guide them to the mountain top. These foreigners came to prove to everyone that the Ark was not there. Instead, Haji's father found it. Angry, the "foreign atheists" tried to destroy the Ark. Failing that, they swore an oath amongst themselves never to reveal this secret, threatening to kill Haji and his father if they ever spoke of the find. Only many years later, and safe in America, did Haji conquer his fears and tell the story. But there is more. Supposedly a newspaper article printed just after World War I mentioned a British scientist, who, on his deathbed, confessed to what the old Armenian had said. He had been one of the "atheists" who attempted to destroy the Ark. Alas, the newspaper article was lost and has never been found.

Modern Expeditions

Sometimes the difficulties of communication can add a touch of humor to the dangerous search for the Ark. On Sept. 12, 1876, James Bryce, British ambassador to the United States and noted historian, found what he believed was Noah's Ark. He was on a vacation climb, done for the sheer challenge of scaling Ararat. Accompanied by a friend, five Cossacks

"There is so much evidence that the Ark is really there."

Geologist John Morris quoted in *Humanist* magazine

"I imagine that after 5,000 years the wood of the Ark, even coated with pitch, has long since returned to dust."

Andre Parrot, *The Flood and Noah's Ark*

(Russian soldiers) on horseback, and four Kurdish guides, he proceeded up the steep sides of the mountain. At 12,000 feet, all but two of the Cossacks and one Kurdish guide flatly refused to go any further.

But Bryce would not let the mountain beat him. He continued onward, eventually climbing along a ridge of solid rock. At 13,000 feet, he reports, "I saw a piece of wood about four feet long and five inches thick, apparently cut by some tool, and so far above the tree line, it couldn't possibly be a tree."

Bryce held it up, shouting "Noah!" Neither the Russian soldiers nor the Kurdish guide spoke or understood English. However they cheerfully shared his excitement. What a sight that must have been!

Cutting off a piece of the wood with his ice ax. Bryce carried it along, continuing his successful climb to the peak. But there is no record of what happened to the wood.

Other Ark Sightings

Forty years later, another Ark find was made. A Russian pilot named Roskovitsky reported seeing from the air the remains of an ancient boat on Ararat's slopes. An enthusiastic Czar soon sent out a search team. The search team stated they found the Ark. Although unable to move it, they made a detailed report. Unfortunately, during the Bolshevik revolution in 1917 the Ark report was lost, and the people involved in the search were scattered. Yet many years later, in stories told by relatives of those soldiers who had been on the expedition, the tale was repeated. Later, stories circulated that the Czar's report still existed in a Swiss library, the gift of a General who may or may not have been in the Czarist Army. However the documents have never been found. Roskovitsky may have just wanted a bit of fame, or he may have incorrectly identified the Ark, or the soldiers with him were perhaps too frightened of the Czar's wrath to search and report

This hull-like depression is where Ark hunter David Fasold believes Noah's vessel came to rest after sliding down the slopes of Mt. Ararat.

finding nothing. On the other hand, something might have been found. If so, were the documents lost, burned, or destroyed in the Russian revolution? Or perhaps the persistent rumors are true, and the Ark reports are still in a library someplace, hidden at the bottom of a pile of ancient yellowed papers.

Another mysterious Ark find, this one just twenty years later, occurred on August 13, 1936. Archaeologist Hardwicke Knight began his Ararat climb. First he was kidnapped by men on horseback. Two days later, without a word being spoken, they released him on the mountain. Having no idea where he was, Knight just kept moving westward, hoping to reach the north face of the mountain.

Did Knight find the Ark on his momentous journey? He didn't think so at the time, but after reaching the bottom of the mountain, he began rethinking what he had seen along the way: timber sticking out of the snow near an area called Ahora Gorge. Ahora Gorge, almost 800 feet of sheer cliff, is located at the melting end of the Black Glacier of the northeastern side of Ararat.

Returning to Ararat and Ahora Gorge thirty years later, Knight and his group searched without success for the timber pieces. Were they once again buried under snow? Had they fallen into Ahora Gorge? Or was it all an illusion of a man lost in the freezing mountains during a blizzard?

Every time an explorer finds proof of the Ark, it seems to disappear. One of the most frustrating instances occurred in 1953 when American mining engineer George Jefferson Greene flew his helicopter over Mount Ararat. He reported clearly seeing a ship's prow in the ice. He circled it several times, getting within ninety feet of the boat, and took many photographs. He developed these upon his return home, making clear enlargements. He showed these enlargements to thirty people. Several of these people later declared the photos unmistakably showed a vessel in the ice, and were neither faked nor altered. One witness even drew a rough sketch of the photo he found most interesting. It showed a large, squarish object on the edge of a sheer cliff, mostly hidden by ice and debris, with visible parallel lines showing wood planking.

These photos might have solved the mystery of Noah's Ark. But the solution escaped us again. Greene went to British Guiana on another mining project and was murdered there in 1962. The murder was never solved. The photographs have never been found.

The Navarra Case

Even more controversy surrounds the 1952 Ark findings of French amateur explorer Fernand Navarra. Like other climbers before him, the ascent was not easy: "After the rough ground, the crest

Formations like this on Mt. Ararat have convinced some Ark hunters that the distinctive ribbing of a ship's hull has been entombed in the slopes.

Parrot Gorge, where melting ice runs deep into a fissure on the northeast side of Ararat. Fernand Navarra claimed that the remnants of the Ark lie covered by glacial ice.

became sharper and sharper, with real razor edges to the rocks on which we cut ourselves when we fell." Navarra began to believe that Ararat was defending itself against intruders, using all possible methods: mountain sickness, rocks, wind, snow, blizzard, altitude. "We wanted to give up and lie down to sleep," he wrote. "We could no longer think. We had only courage to breathe once more so as to take one step forward. We could not stop, we would not sleep, we had no right to quit!"

Navarra's group pressed on, sucking ice to relieve their thirst, crawling on their hands and knees. pulling each other along. Into the twilight they went, and then "we reached the summit of Noah's Mountain, the Holy Mountain, the Cradle of Humanity."

Triumphant, exhausted, surrounded by a heavenly

world of white, they expected nothing more. And then they looked down. "Beneath our eyes was this astonishing patch of blackness within the ice, its outlines sharply defined."

Their energies flared by excitement, Navarra and his companions began to trace the shape of the patch on foot. There were two long incurving lines, about 500 feet each, meeting in the heart of the glacier. "The shape was unmistakably that of a ship's hull!" he reported. Only a few yards of ice separated Navarra and his companions from one of humanity's most important discoveries. But a few yards of ice seemed like a million miles of it without sophisticated equipment. Navarra was forced to leave his find behind him.

A year later he returned with photographic equip-

This photograph of eastern Turkey was taken by the Earth Resources Technology Satellite (ERTS-1). The snow-capped peak in the lower portion of the photograph is Mt. Ararat. Some "Ark-eologists" believe that secret aerial photographs exist that would provide the Ark's exact location.

Modern technology has been employed to detect traces of wood, metal and other ship-building materials beneath the slopes of Mt. Ararat.

ment, only to be forced down by severe mountain sickness before reaching the summit. Undaunted, some months later he returned, bringing his 11-year-old son Raphael to aid in carrying equipment. This time they reached the spot where Navarra had seen the ship under ice.

Lowering himself into an ice crevice with a rope ladder, Navarra claims to have seen wooden beams, wood that was evenly cut and obviously hand tooled. With much difficulty, he hacked off a piece of dark, hand-worked, fossilized wood five feet long.

Navarra's wood caused a public and scientific sensation. To prove or disprove its authenticity, it was subjected to all kinds of international tests, including carbon-14 dating.

Carbon-14 dating is widely used to date objects derived from once living materials such as wood, animals, and plants. The carbon-14 tests are based on the fact that every plant or animal absorbs a certain amount of radioactive carbon from the atmosphere during its lifetime. When the plant or animal dies, carbon supplies are cut off. Fossil or plant age is estimated using a process which shows how much radioactive carbon remains. The fossils or plants with the least carbon-14 remaining are the oldest. Navarra's wood was analyzed at the Cairo Museum in Egypt, the University of Bordeaux in France, and the Forestry Institute of Research and Experimentation in Madrid, Spain.

The Egyptian report gave a 5,000- to 6000-year-old date. The French report said the wood "came from a very long, long time ago." The Spanish analysis said the wood fragment was 5,000 years old, dating back to the same time as the Great Flood. Later, other studies using radioactive carbon-14 tests done by both England's National Physics Laboratory in the 1960s and the University of California at Los Angeles in 1970s date Navarra's wood at only 1,200 to 1,400 years old. A University of Pennsylvania test put it at a mere 560 years old. The extremely wide age-date variation found in the scientific analysis could be due to many factors: the skill of the scientists, the specific tests done, the equipment used, or any hardships the wood might have undergone during its travels. Creationists claim that exposure to an unusual amount of cosmic rays due to Ararat's altitude affected the test results. The true date of Navarra's wood was surely 4300 B.C., the date of Noah's Flood, they say.

What might Navarra's wood be if not Ark wood? UCLA archaeologist Rainer Berger guessed the wood might be pieces of a pilgrim's shrine or monument marking an Ark landing near that site. A relationship to the Ark legend is considered likely even

"If the Ark of Noah is ever discovered, it would be the greatest archaeological find in human history, the greatest event since the resurrection of Christ, and it would alter all the currents of scientific thought."

Melvin Grosvenor, editor of *National Geographic* magazine

"We know the Ark is there."

Astronaut and ark hunter James Irwin, quoted in *Maclean's* magazine by skeptics, but what that relationship might be is yet another mystery.

Are There Photographs of the Ark?

Some people believe that absolute proof of the Ark's existence has been found but is being kept secret. Authors Tim LaHaye and John Morris have suggested that there may be classified military photos of the Ark. They write, "We have learned of three distinct sets of military photographs taken of Mt. Ararat, two of which are reported to show the Ark."

However LaHaye and Morris have been unable to acquire these photos. "In order to obtain Defense photographs of Mt. Ararat," LaHaye and Morris state, "one must first obtain a release from the Turkish Department of Interior and the military hierarchy, to say the least, a mammoth task, but not an impossible one."

"Meanwhile," Dr. John Morris wrote in 1988, "efforts are continuing to evaluate recent high resolution satellite imagery of Mount Ararat. Computer enhancement techniques makes it possible to 'see' objects as little as three meters in diameter." The results are not yet in.

Many Ark Hunters Are Still Optimistic

"Arkeologists," as Ark hunters are sometimes called, insist the Ark is on Ararat and that it is merely a matter of time before someone finds it. As Dr. Morris writes: "In spite of the volcanic eruptions, the earthquakes, the erosion of the glacier, and the effects of time, the data strongly assert that the remains of the Ark lie somewhere on Mount Ararat, buried by volcanic debris and ice, awaiting the proper time."

Arkeologist Rene Noorbergen is one of a handful of modern researchers who believe the Ark is not located near the summit of Ararat but is in a valley below the mountain. They cite evidence of an ancient volcanic mud flow that swept the ancient craft down the slopes and brought it to rest away from the popular search sites. David Fasold, author of *The Ark of Noah*, has used radar detection equipment to reveal what he claims is the outline of a boat matching the Biblical dimensions of the Ark. He claims the boat is now petrified; that is, it has been turned to stone by time and weathering. This theory, published in 1988, is so recent that other scholars have not tested Fasold's hypothesis.

The only statement that can be made with certainty is that many people have claimed from ancient times that the Ark has been found, yet the site has continued to remain elusive, shifting all around the slopes of Ararat like a ghost.

Conclusion

The Search Goes On

While Noah's Ark may seem merely a fascinating story to some, the battles over which viewpoint is correct have become extremely noisy at times. Opinions are divided into three main factions, each of whom consider themselves completely correct: Noah's Flood *did* occur; The Flood did *not* occur; The Flood *may* have occurred. Will we ever know the truth?

The Flood Did Occur

Strict biblical interpreters state Noah's Ark and the universal Flood happened exactly as described in Genesis. Creationists, or creation scientists (as many prefer being called), do not believe evolution occurred. Instead, the Creator set aside six days, and in that time made the world and every type of animal and plant in it. Humans have always been humans, elephants have always been elephants, and ants ants. The mountains, canyons, petrified forests, fossil beds, and coal and oil deposits cannot have developed over billions of years because the earth, according to the book of Genesis, is just 6,000 years old.

Instead of evolutionary processes, earth's uneven

"The grand fact of a universal deluge at no very remote period is proved on grounds so decisive and incontrovertible, that had we never heard of such an event from Scripture or any other Authority, Geology of itself must have called in the assistance of some such catastrophe to explain the phenomena of diluvial action."

Professor William Buckland quoted by W.J. Sollas in The Age of the Earth

"The idea of a universal deluge, or even of closely connected but local deluges on a large scale cannot, I think, claim any real support from geology."

Professor T.G. Booney, Science and the Flood

surface and fossil remnants came about because of God-sent catastrophes. A universal Flood changed land shape, climate, and animal living places. Many scholars quoted in this book have done much research to prove that Genesis, including the universal Deluge, occurred as stated in the Bible. Sometimes current discovery does not fit precisely with biblical statements. But that, according to creationists, is not because the Bible is wrong, but because people have not yet learned to interpret the Bible's words correctly.

Current creationist researchers state: (1) archaeology has proven parts of the Bible to be historically accurate; (2) fossil evidence exists for a great Deluge; (3) environmental conditions were once present which could have produced universal flood; (4) all facts and figures confirm that Noah and his family could have built a ship as described in the Bible, that it would have held the animals mentioned, and that it would have safely survived the Flood.

Witnesses claim to have seen Noah's Ark, remnants of it, on Mount Ararat. Some say there is actual physical and photographic proof of the Ark's existence. Only political conflicts, combined with bad weather, terrible terrain, and difficult climbing conditions, have kept the Ark on Ararat a secret.

Physicist Gerald Aardsma states, "What I'm asserting is that you will never find science proving Scripture wrong."

The Flood Did Not Occur

Skeptics state there could never have been a universal Flood. There is no *undisputed* geological, fossil, or archaeological evidence of a universal Flood. Many question the huge amount of water necessary to produce such a Flood. If the highest mountains in the world are 29,000 feet high, and flood waters covered the entire earth, over 116 bil-

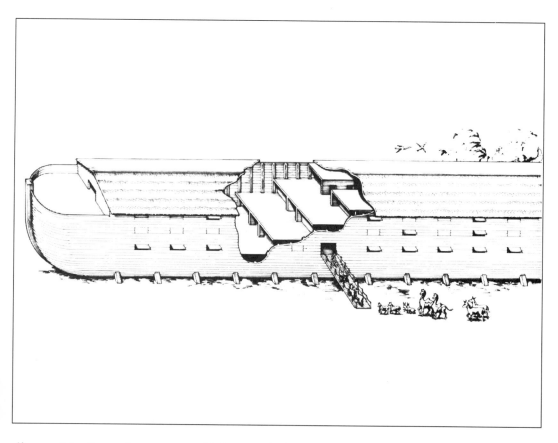

lion cubic feet of water would be needed. Would forty days and forty nights of rain provide all the necessary water?

Skeptics of the Noah story also say the Ark would be too small for all those animals. They question Noah's ability to get two of every kind from all over the world. They want to know how animals from the freezing Arctic region could survive for an entire year on the same boat with animals from tropical areas. They also mention the lack of food storage space on the Ark, the smell of animal waste, etc. If given answers to these question, only then would they believe the Ark existed as described in the Bible.

The construction of the Ark is just one of many points debated by biblical scholars.

Ark hunter James Irwin displays a Turkish newspaper showing him recovering in a hospital. He was injured while attempting to climb Mt. Ararat.

The Flood May Have Occured

There is a vast middle ground between those stating the biblical description is completely accurate and those denying the existence of Noah and the universal Flood. Scholars in this middle ground say there *may* have been a Flood, but it probably did not occur exactly as the Bible describes it.

As far back as 1895, English geologist T.G. Bonney asked about the chronology of the Bible. He did not doubt there may have been a major flood, be he believed "the flood thus produced would be many thousand years before the time" the Deluge was supposed to have taken place. The text *Insight on the Scriptures*, published in 1988 by the Watch Tower Bible and Tract Society of New York and the International Bible Students Association, suggests that there may be some misinterpretation of biblical time as stated in Genesis. The "flexible use of the word 'day' to express units of time of varying lengths is clearly evident in the Genesis account of Creation," according to this book. "The Bible does not specify the length of each of the creative periods." This means the "days" of the Bible may be much longer than our current 24-hour-day.

The Bible itself, 2 Peter 3.8, states "that one day with the Lord is as a thousand years, and a thousand years as one day." If one day is equal to a thousand years, or another time figure not yet discovered, people who doubt the Flood because they don't believe it occurred just 4,300 years ago might have reason to change their viewpoint.

Another source of confusion is the hundreds of different Flood tales. Some persons dismiss them all as myths. Others say they may have some truth but are not in any way related to the biblical story.

"We must conclude that the Flood story is an old tradition, going back to the end of the Stone Age before the present bounds of the oceans were fixed," says author G. E. Wright. "To place the tradition this early would make it possible for us to account for the widespread diffusion over the earth of so many different versions of a catastrophe by flood."

There are also those who believe there were many floods. "Though stories of such tremendous cataclysms are almost certainly fabulous," says author and historian James Frazer, "it is possible and indeed probable that under a mythical husk many of them may hide a kernel of truth." Perhaps, Frazer continues, they may contain memories of floods which really overtook some areas. With the passage of time, the memories became distorted. The original event might not even be recognizable.

"Even the traditions of a purely local flood," Frazer says, "in which many people had been drowned, might unconsciously be exaggerated into

"Essentially the Bible is neither a historical nor a scientific textbook. It is an account of God's dealing with man, and in the final analysis, its truths spring from faith."

G.S. Wegener, *6,000 Years of the Bible*

"Further excavation and analysis should be pursued with the best scientific methodology available. There is no room for fantasizing."

Explorer Ron Wyatt, quoted in *Christianity Today*

Devil's Rock, one of the many beautiful formations on Mt. Ararat that is frequently mistaken for the Ark itself.

vast dimensions by a European settler or traveller, who received it from savages and interpreted it in the light of the biblical Flood."

In the region around Ararat, Frazer says, there may have been an extremely destructive water flow resulting in the Sumerian legend. For example, even in modern times, floods caused by melting snow can still endanger the lower river valleys. Disastrous flash floods are common throughout Bible lands, where long dry spells are followed by extremely heavy rains. Frazer seems to feel that the great floods would be regional ones, rather than worldwide.

The experts debate each other. For every "fact" one has, another comes up with a different "fact," all or most based on scholarly research. But researchers put facts together in different, and often opposing, ways.

Hundreds of books and articles have been written about Noah, the Ark, and the universal Deluge.

Opinions come from archaeologists, geologists, paleontologists, biologists, explorers, authors, historians, creationists, biblical scholars, and those who are just plain fascinated by the tale of eight brave people riding out a massive flood on a huge wooden ship while the wicked world around them perished. But no one has yet discovered the unarguable truth.

No doubt the debate about Noah, the Ark, and the universal Deluge will continue until someone invents a way to travel back in time, or until one method of verification is acknowledged by all scientists.

The awesome power of the Flood, and God's will, is forever remembered in wall paintings and engravings around the world.

Glossary

Aboriginal inhabiting a country from the earliest known times

Archaeology the science which investigates the history of ancient peoples by the remains belonging to the earliest periods of their existence

Artifact ordinary items, such as tools or ornaments, showing human workmanship

Canopy a roof-like projection or covering

Cubit an ancient measuring unit, usually translated as seventeen to twenty-one inches

Cuneiform having the shape of a wedge, or written in wedge-shaped characters; and ancient form of writing

Deluge a great flood or overflowing of water

Epic an extended narrative poem, typically centered upon a hero, and describing extraordinary achievements and events

Evolution the theory of the descent of all living things from a few simple forms of life, or from a single form

Excavate to expose or lay bare by digging

Extinct the end of a species

Fossil remains or other traces of past animals and plants that have been preserved, or saved, over the ages.

Fundamentalist one who believes the Bible is to be accepted literally as a spiritual and historical document that is never wrong

Geology the science that deals with the physical history and structure of the earth and the physical changes which it has undergone or is undergoing

Legend a story or account that is handed down by tradition from earlier times and popularly accepted as factual, though there is no proof that it happened

Myth any invented story; something or someone having no existence in fact

Paleontology the biological science that deals with fossil remains
Petrified converted into a stony substance
Pitch various dark and thick liquid substances used for sealing the seams of wooden vessels

Sediment material deposited by water, wind, or glaciers
Scourge a punishment or affliction
Skeptic one who disbelieves or hesitates to believe

For Further Exploration

Dave Balsinger and Charles E. Sellier, Jr., *In Search of Noah's Ark*. California: Sun Classic Books, 1976.

Charles Berlitz, *The Lost Ship of Noah*. New York: G.P. Putnam's Sons, 1987.

C.M. Bowra, *Classical Greece*. New York: Time-Life Books (Great Ages of Man).

Sir James George Frazer, *Folklore in the Old Testament*. London: Macmillan, 1918.

Michael Harrison and Christopher Stuart-Clark, *Noah's Ark*. London: Oxford University Press, 1984.

Samuel Noah Kramer, *Cradle of Civilization*. New York: Time-Life Books (Great Ages of Man).

Tim La Haye & John Morris, *The Ark on Ararat*. New York: Thomas Nelson, 1976.

John Warwick Montgomery, *The Quest for Noah's Ark*. Minnesota: Dimension Books, 1975.

James B. Pritchard, *Archaeology and the Old Testament*. New Jersey: Princeton University Press, 1958.

World Mythology, An Encyclopedia. New York: Galahad Books, 1975.

Additional Bibliography

Books

Alan Dundes, *The Flood Myth*. Berkeley: University of California Press, 1988.

Jack Finegan, *Archaeological History of the Ancient Middle East*. New York: Dorset Press, 1979.

Lloyd Graham, *Deceptions and Myths of the Bible*. New York: Bell Publishing, 1979.

Edith Hamilton, *Mythology*. New York: New American Library, 1969.

Alexander Hcidcl, *The Gilgamesh Epic and Old Testament Parallels*. University of Chicago Press, 1949.

David Lambert, *Field Guide to Geology*. New York: Facts on File, 1988.

Madeleine S. Miller and J. Lane Miller, *Harper's Encyclopedia of Bible Life*. San Francisco: Harper & Row, 1976.

My Book of Bible Stories, Watch Tower Bible and Tract Society of Pennsylvania, 1978.

André Parrot, *The Flood and Noah's Ark*. London: SCM Press Ltd., 1955, in translation.

Moshe Pearlman, *Digging up the Bible*. New York: William Morrow & Co., 1980.

Periodicals

Ann Bahar. "Only On Sunday," *Antiques &
Collecting,* April 1986, p. 46-48.

Sarah Boxer. "Will Creationism Rise Again?,"
Discover, October 1987, p. 80-86.

Robert Brow. "Late-Date Genesis Man,"
Christianity Today, Sept. 15, 1972, p. 6-7.

J.W. Burrow. "The Flood," *Horizon*, Summer 1972.

Jared Diamond. "Voyage of the Overloaded Ark,"
Discover, June 1985, p.82-92.

Cesare Emiliani. "The Great Flood," *Sea Frontiers*,
Sept-Oct. 1976, p. 260-270.

Gordon Gaskill. "The Mystery of Noah's Ark,"
Readers Digest, Sept. 1975, p. 150-155.

Arthur Gaunt. "Ararat's Mystery Ship," *Sea
Frontiers*, May-June, 1977, p. 167-171.

Martin E. Marty. "Noah and the Arkeologists,"
Christian Century, Nov. 1976, p. 1063.

John Morris. "A Report on the ICR Ararat
Exploration, 1987," *Impact*, January 1988.

Pat Ohlendorf. "Noah's Ark and Biblical Truth,"
Maclean's, Oct. 25, 1982, p. 60.

Rev. Stuart A. Parvin. "Noah's Ark," *Hobbies,* Oct. 1970, p. 158- 59.

Wesley G. Pippert. "Boat from First Century is Discovered at Sea of Galilee," *Christianity Today,* Nov. 1986, p. 86.

Leonard G. Soroka and Charles L. Nelson. "Physical Constraints on the Noachian Deluge," Journal of Geological Education, 1983, v. 31.

Robert Yoakum. "Noah Confuses History Class," *Humanist,* Nov./Dec. 1982, p. 51.

"A Question of Credentials," (Montgomery/Lenton), *Christianity Today*, Aug. 27, 1971, p. 15.

"Ararat 'Ark' Wood Dated at A.D. 700," *Science News,* Vol. 11, March 26, 1977, p. 198-99.

"Ark Fever," *Christianity Today*, July 2, 1961, p. 38-39.

"Did They Find Noah's Ark? Explorers Can't Agree," *Christianity Today*, Oct. 5, 1984, p. 71.

"Eighth Century Ark," *Scientific American*, July 1980.

"Excavations at Nippur," *National Geographic*, Oct.1900, p. 392.

"Expedition Seeks to Recover Remains of Noah's Ark," *Christian Century*, Jan. 2, 1970, p. 72.

"In the Wake of the Ark," *Science News,* 1970,
   Vol. 7, p. 574.

"Noah's Liberty Ship," *Time* magazine, Feb. 23,
   1968, p. 76-78.

"Search for Noah's Ark Continues," *Acts & Facts,*
   Vol 17, Nov. 1988, p. 4.

Index

About the Author

Patricia Kite, a freelance writer and journalism instructor, has a dual background in biological science and journalism. She holds a B.S. from U.C. Medical Center in San Francisco, a life teaching credential in Biology and Social Science, and a M.S. in Mass Communications and Journalism from San Jose State University in California.

Patricia has written for newspapers, magazines, and business publications on a wide variety of topics. Currently she specializes in science for children and adults. She has written books on insects and carnivorous plants, as well as contemporary fiction.

Patricia has four daughters, Rachel, Karen, Laura and Sally, two dogs, Lady and Muzzy, plus Toby Bear, a Siamese cat. She enjoys travelling, walking long distances, gardening, reading, and being curious.

Picture Credits